Better Homes and Gardens®

STEP-BY-STEP

Outdoor
Projects

Better Homes and Gardens® Books
Des Moines, Iowa

Better Homes and Gardens® Books
An imprint of Meredith® Books

Step-by-Step Outdoor Projects
Editor: Paula Marshall
Associate Art Director: Lynda Haupert
Contributing Copy Editors: Melinda Levine, James Sanders
Contributing Proofreaders: Jeanette Alt, Debra Morris Smith, Margaret Smith
Technical Proofreader: Ken Wilkinson
Copy Chief: Catherine Hamrick
Copy and Production Editor: Terri Fredrickson
Electronic Production Coordinator: Paula Forest
Editorial and Design Assistants: Kaye Chabot, Treesa Landry, Karen Schirm
Production Director: Douglas M. Johnston
Production Manager: Pam Kvitne
Assistant Prepress Manager: Marjorie J. Schenkelberg

Produced by Greenleaf Publishing, Inc.
Publishing Director: Dave Toht
Writer: Steve Cory
Editorial Art Director: Jean DeVaty
Assistant Editor: Rebecca JonMichaels
Design: Melanie Lawson Design
Illustrations: Dick Ticcioni, Dick Skover, Art Factory; Greg Maxon, Tony Davis

Cover Photograph: Tony Kubat Photography
Cover Production and Back Cover Design: John Seid

Meredith® Books
Editor in Chief: James D. Blume
Design Director: Matt Strelecki
Managing Editor: Gregory H. Kayko
Executive Shelter Editor: Denise L. Caringer

Director, Sales & Marketing, Retail: Michael A. Peterson
Director, Sales & Marketing, Special Markets: Rita McMullen
Director, Sales & Marketing, Home & Garden Center Channel: Ray Wolf
Director, Operations: George A. Susral
Vice President, General Manager: Jamie L. Martin

Better Homes and Gardens® Magazine
Editor in Chief: Jean LemMon
Executive Building Editor: Joan McCloskey

Meredith Publishing Group
President, Publishing Group: Christopher Little
Vice President, Consumer Marketing & Development: Hal Oringer

Meredith Corporation
Chairman and Chief Executive Officer: William T. Kerr
Chairman of the Executive Committee: E. T. Meredith III

All of us at Better Homes and Gardens® Books are dedicated to providing you with
information and ideas you need to enhance your home. We welcome your comments and
suggestions about this book of outdoor projects. Write to us at: Better Homes and Gardens®
Books, Do-It-Yourself Editorial Department, 1716 Locust St., Des Moines, IA 50309–3023.

Note to the Reader: Due to differing conditions, tools, and individual skills, Meredith
Corporation assumes no responsibility for any damages, injuries suffered, or losses incurred
as a result of following the information published in this book. Before beginning any project,
review the instructions carefully, and if any doubts or questions remain, consult local experts
or authorities. Because local codes and regulations vary greatly, you always should check
with local authorities to ensure that your project complies with all applicable local codes and
regulations. Always read and observe all of the safety precautions provided by any tool or
equipment manufacturer, and follow all accepted safety procedures.

TABLE OF CONTENTS

INTRODUCTION

Outdoor projects offer the rare advantage of being affordable projects that improve the value and livability of your home while minimally disrupting your household. Because they are outdoors, you can dabble at them without the pressure of creating a mess the rest of the household must live with.

Most outdoor projects are also fun to build. The materials are relatively simple to work with and forgiving of minor mistakes. They seldom have to do with plumbing or electrical work where special skills are required and safety concerns are tantamount.

Step-by-Step Outdoor Projects provides the information you need to plan and carry out nearly 40 outdoor projects. Each is within the range of do-it-yourselfers with average skills. You will learn how to plan the project, how to lay it out and provide adequate footings, how to decide which types of materials to use in different installations, and how to finish and maintain your project so it will provide years of service and enjoyment.

Step-by-Step Outdoor Projects helps you decide which jobs you can take on yourself. Even if you decide not to do the job yourself, you will be better equipped to manage the job wisely. Reputable landscaping contractors and carpenters appreciate working with an educated client. If you choose to hire out the job, you will have the knowledge to find the right contractor, choose the right materials, and get the results you want.

Working to Code

Even though you may be an amateur working on your own house and yard, you have the same responsibilities as any contractor. Any structure you build must be solid and long-lasting, as well as square and straight, and must be constructed of material appropriate to the job. That means using only those techniques and materials that are acceptable to the building codes in your area.

Working with Your Local Building Department

Although a modest project, such as building an Adirondack chair, will not require a permit, a permanent structure, such as a fence or shed, likely will. If you are not sure, play it safe and contact your municipal building department.

The procedures in this book represent widely accepted techniques and materials, but be aware that local building codes can vary a great deal. Although they may seem bothersome, codes exist to ensure that minimal standards of quality and safety are met. Ignoring codes can lead to costly mistakes, health hazards, and even difficulties in someday selling your home. Neglecting to check with your building department could cause you the expense and trouble of tearing out and redoing your work.

There's no telling what kind of advice you will encounter when you apply for a permit or when your project is inspected. You may be told that a permit and inspections will not be required. If a permit is needed, you probably will have to have an inspector look at your work. Some inspectors are helpful, friendly, and flexible; others are real sticklers. Regardless of the inspector you get, your work will go better if you follow these guidelines:

■ This book is a good place to start, but learn as much as you can about each project before you talk with an inspector from your local building department. You will avoid miscommunication and get your permits more quickly. Your building department may have literature concerning your type of installation.

■ Go to your building department with a plan to be approved or amended; don't expect the department's staff to plan the job for you. Present your plan with neatly drawn diagrams and a complete list of the materials you will be using.

■ Be sure you understand clearly when you need to have inspections. Do not cover up any work that needs to be inspected.

■ Be as courteous as possible. Inspectors often are wary of homeowners' work, so show the inspector you are serious about doing things the right way and comply with any requirements.

How to Use This Book

B egin by browsing the projects found on pages 20 through 107 of this book. They are divided into five sections: "Fences and Gates," "Arbors, Overheads, and Trellises," "Seating and Planters," "Sheds and Play Structures," and "Exterior Improvements." Choose the ones that interest you and then check the section "Tools and Materials" for specific information on what you'll need before beginning your project.

In addition, review the skills presented in "Basic Techniques." Here you will be given a brief apprenticeship in the essential skills you'll need to complete your outdoor project.

Feature Boxes

I n addition to basic instructions, you'll find plenty of tips throughout this book. For every project, a You'll Need box tells you how long the project will take, what skills are necessary, and what tools you must have. The other tip boxes shown on this page are scattered throughout the book, providing practical help to ensure the outdoor projects you do will be as pleasurable as possible, and that it will result in safe, long-lasting improvements to your home and yard.

EXPERTS' INSIGHT

Tricks of the trade can make all the difference in helping you do a job quickly and well. Experts' Insight gives you insiders' tips on how to make the job easier.

TOOLS TO USE

If you'll need special tools not commonly found in a homeowner's toolbox, we'll tell you about them in Tools to Use.

Money Saver

Throwing money at a job does not necessarily make it a better one. Money Saver helps cut your costs with tips on how to accurately estimate your material needs, make wise tool purchases, and organize the job to minimize wasted labor.

MEASUREMENTS

Keep an eye out for this box when standard measurements, critical tolerances, or special measuring techniques are called for.

CAUTION!
When a how-to step requires special care, Caution! warns you what to watch out for. It will help keep you from doing damage to yourself or the job at hand.

SELECTING BASIC TOOLS

The right tool makes your job much easier and helps yield better results. Top-of-the-line contractor-type tools are of higher quality than an average homeowner needs. On the other hand, bargain-bin tools do not perform well. In most cases, your best choice is a midpriced model. However, if you need an unusual tool for a single task, go with a cheaper version or rent it.

A **tape measure** will see plenty of action. Buy a 25-footer with a 1-inch-wide tape; this will extend farther and last longer than a ¾-inch tape. Use a **framing square** (also called a carpenter's square) to check corners for square and to mark for rafters. A **triangular speed square** is easy to use, allows you to mark quickly for 90- and 45-degree-angle cuts, and holds its shape after getting banged around. Some carpenters prefer a **combination square,** because its length can be adjusted. A **T-bevel** can be set to duplicate an angle.

Plumb and level large and small projects with a **carpenter's level.** A 4-foot model works well for most projects. Use a **line level** to check for level over a long distance—it hangs on a string. Suspend a **plumb bob** to establish true vertical lines. Snap long, straight lines with a **chalk line.** A chalk line can also double as a plumb bob. Have plenty of pencils on hand. Some do-it-yourselfers prefer a flat **carpenter's pencil,** that lasts a long time between sharpenings, while others prefer the finer line of a standard pencil.

A **handsaw** often comes in handy for small cuts or for cuts in awkward places. A **circular saw** is the tool you'll use most often for cutting; it easily crosscuts, angle-cuts, rips (cuts lengthwise), and even bevels lumber. Choose one that takes 7¼-inch blades. If it is

rated at 12 or more amps and runs on ball bearings, it will last longer and make smoother cuts than a cheaper model. Many good saws have plastic housings. For curved cuts, use a **sabersaw.** Consider one with variable speed. A sabersaw pulling 3 amps or more handles most difficult jobs.

Buy a **hammer** that is comfortable and built solidly. The most popular model weighs 16 ounces and has a curved claw. Use a **nail set** to sink the heads of finishing nails below the surface of the wood. **Wood chisels** let you make notches in places where a saw will not reach; choose chisels with metal-capped handles. Keep your **utility knife** in your tool belt; you'll be surprised how often it comes in handy.

Don't try to work without a **variable-speed, reversible power drill.** You can use it for drilling holes and driving screws. Get one that pulls at least 3.5 amps, with a ⅜-inch chuck. A keyless chuck makes changing bits quick and easy, but some people prefer a keyed chuck for a tighter grip on the bit. A **cordless drill** is portable but less suited to heavy drilling. Get a set of **twist bits,** ranging from ¹⁄₁₆ to ¼ inch, as well as **spade bits** for larger holes. To drill holes in concrete or brick purchase a **masonry bit.**

To fasten nuts, bolts, and lag screws, use an **adjustable wrench.** A pair of **tongue-and-groove pliers** is a great all-purpose tool. A pair of **locking pliers** holds pieces tight while you work. Have on hand a couple of sizes of **Phillips** and **standard screwdrivers.**

Clamps of various shapes and sizes hold pieces of wood firmly together. **C-clamps** hold best; **squeeze clamps** fasten quickly. Use an **adjustable clamp** when needed for holding several pieces of lumber.

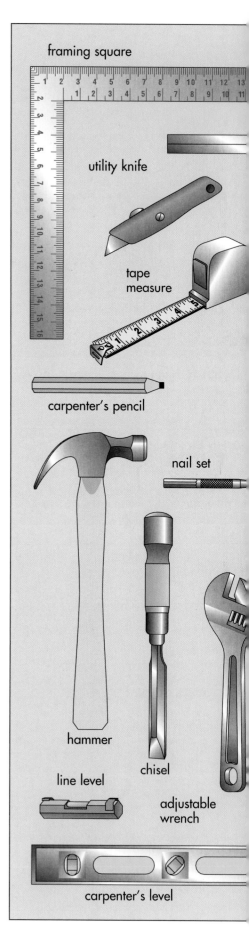

framing square

utility knife

tape measure

carpenter's pencil

nail set

hammer

line level

chisel

adjustable wrench

carpenter's level

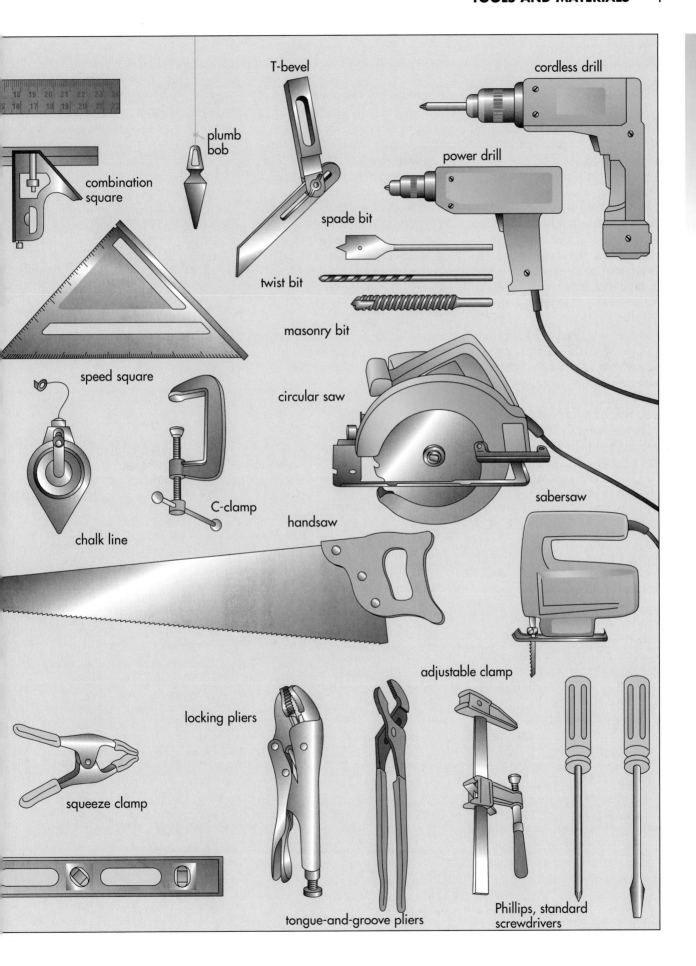

T-bevel

cordless drill

plumb
bob

power drill

combination
square

spade bit

twist bit

masonry bit

speed square

circular saw

sabersaw

chalk line

C-clamp

handsaw

adjustable clamp

locking pliers

squeeze clamp

tongue-and-groove pliers

Phillips, standard
screwdrivers

SELECTING SPECIALIZED TOOLS

Outdoor projects go easier with the help of some specialized tools. Power tools can be very expensive, so do some research before buying. If the tool is one you will use often, invest in a high-quality one that will last. If you will use it only rarely, settle for a lesser quality tool or rent it. In most cases, a tool with ball bearings and high amperage is the better tool. A plastic housing does not necessarily mean poor quality.

If you want professional-looking cuts, choose among three tools. A **tablesaw** is great for making straight, long cuts and for dado cuts as well. Choose one with a solid table that won't wiggle as you work, a fence that adjusts smoothly and stays firmly in place, and a powerful motor. You need a lot of room in your shop if you plan to use a tablesaw to cut plywood.

A **power miter saw,** also called a chopsaw or cutoff saw, will make quick and precise crosscuts and miter cuts. Get one that is large enough to cut all the way through the stock you want to cut; a 10-inch blade handles most projects.

A **radial-arm saw** is a general-purpose tool. It makes long cuts like a tablesaw and crosscuts and miter cuts like a power miter saw.

Only a high-quality model will produce precise cuts, and it takes more time to operate. However, if you have limited space, this may be your best choice.

Digging postholes is often the most difficult part of an outdoor project. A **clamshell posthole digger** works for digging post or footing holes as long as the soil is worked fairly easily. For heavier jobs, you may want to hire a landscaping company to dig the holes for you or you may want to rent a **power auger.** When setting posts, a **post level** makes it easy to check for plumb in both directions.

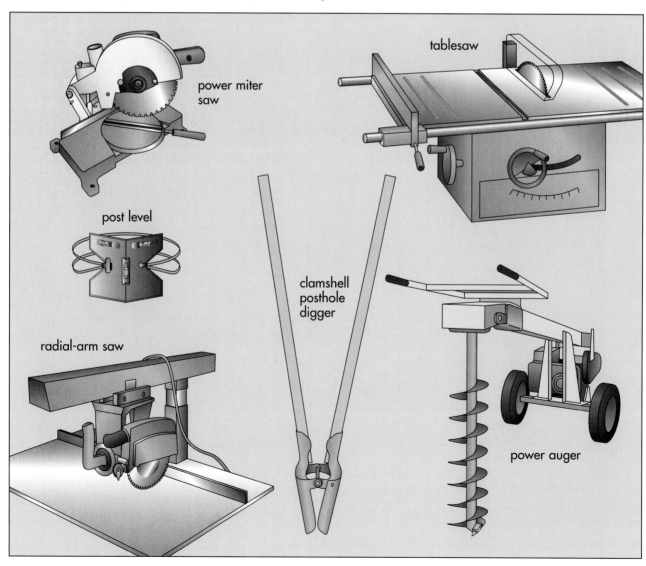

power miter saw

tablesaw

post level

clamshell posthole digger

radial-arm saw

power auger

CHOOSING HARDWARE

A large number of hardware options are available for outdoor projects. If you have an unusual fastening problem, check with your local home center or hardware store; chances are good they will have the solution.

Gates are usually heavy and need large hinges fastened with long screws. Before choosing either a **strap hinge** or a **T-hinge**, make sure the hinge fits your situation—you want to be able to drive all the screws into solid wood. A **screw-hook hinge** is a good solution when you don't need the hinge to be showy. Install a **gate spring** if you want the gate to close automatically.

If your structure calls for posts that are not sunk in the ground, choose a fastening method that raises them off the concrete a bit to prevent rot. Often, you will need to set a **J-bolt** in the wet concrete of a footing before you can attach a **post anchor.** To attach a beam to a post, use a **post cap. Joist hangers** enable you to attach ends of joists to a ledger board firmly.

Choose fasteners that will hold firmly and not rust. Galvanized-and-coated **deck screws** make great all-purpose fasteners. (If you're working with redwood or cedar, use stainless steel screws to prevent discoloring the wood.) To attach wood to concrete, use **lag shields** with screws for the strongest connection. **Masonry screws** are easier to install and almost as strong. Use **lag screws** for heavy-duty fastening. **Machine bolts** have a head that can be turned with a wrench. (Always use washers when installing lag screws or machine bolts, or their heads will get buried in the wood.) Use a **carriage bolt** when you want a dressier look on one side.

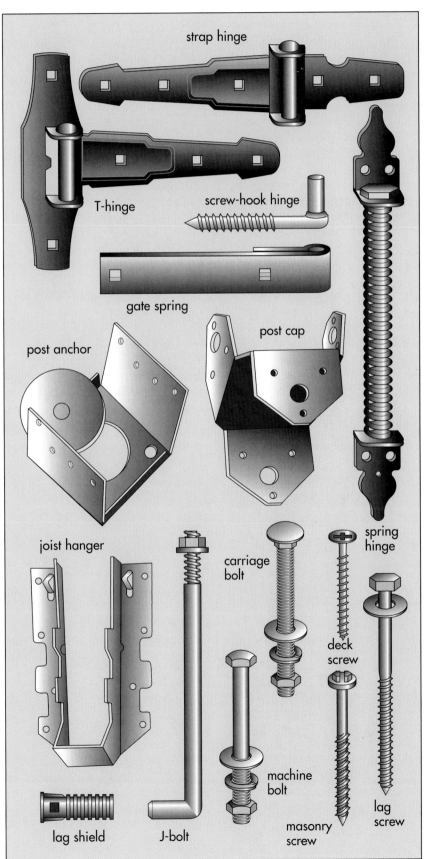

strap hinge

T-hinge

screw-hook hinge

gate spring

post anchor

post cap

spring hinge

joist hanger

carriage bolt

deck screw

machine bolt

lag screw

lag shield

J-bolt

masonry screw

CHOOSING LUMBER

For outdoor projects, you will most likely use softwood, made from coniferous trees, rather than hardwood, made from deciduous trees. Choose wood that will not rot: either pressure-treated lumber or the heartwood of cedar or redwood.

Wood is graded according to how many knots it has and the quality of its surface. There are a variety of grading systems. Here are some of the most common designations: *Clear* lumber has no knots. *Select* or *select structural* is high quality, with few knots. *Number 2 common* has tight knots and no major blemishes, while *number 3 common* contains loose knots or other blemishes. *Construction, standard,* and *utility* all designate economy-grade lumber that should be used for rough framing only.

Watch out for the types of wood problems shown at right. A piece of lumber that is heavily twisted, bowed, cupped, or crooked usually is not usable, although you can often correct minor problems as you nail the boards in place. Checking, which is a rift on the surface, is only cosmetic. On the other hand, splits cannot be repaired and will widen in time. Cut them off.

Actual dimensions of lumber differ from the nominal dimensions. For instance, when you ask for a 2×4 you'll get a board 1½ inches by 3½ inches; a nominal 1×6 will measure ¾ inch by 5½ inches.

Plywood is commonly used for flooring, siding, and decking under roofing. Plywood is strong because it is made of laminated layers running in perpendicular directions. Use pressure-treated plywood if it will be exposed to moisture or near the ground.

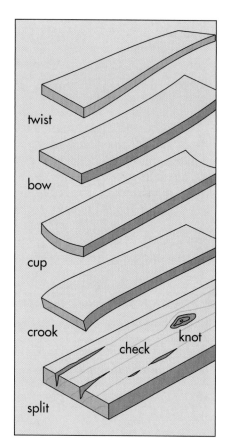

twist

bow

cup

crook

check

knot

split

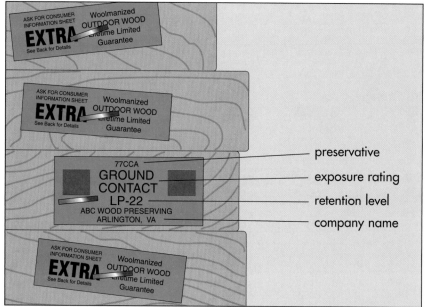

preservative

exposure rating

retention level

company name

Check your pressure-treated wood. Choose pressure-treated lumber with a preservative retention level of .40 or more. This may be indicated on the label as *LP-22* or *ground contact*. Whether green- or brown-treated, the best preservative is *cca*, chromated copper arsenate. Although toxic, this chemical is dangerous only while lumber is being cut or while it is still wet with preservative. When cutting such lumber wear a respirator and gloves.

CAUTION!
REDWOOD AND CEDAR SAPWOOD WILL ROT

Just because you've spent the money for redwood or cedar doesn't mean you are free from worries about rot. The heartwood of these species, usually dark in color, is extremely resistant to rot. But cedar and the sapwood of redwood (typically creamy in color) will rot if exposed to moisture.

When you buy redwood, the designation common *means there is sapwood present;* heart *or* all heart *means heartwood. For cedar, you have to look at the board—the darker it is, the more rot resistant it will be.*

You may be able to buy treated redwood, which will be rot resistant even though it contains sapwood. Heartwood of cedar increasingly is difficult to find, so your best bet is to use cedar in places where it can dry out between rainfalls, and to treat it with a preservative (see pages 18–19).

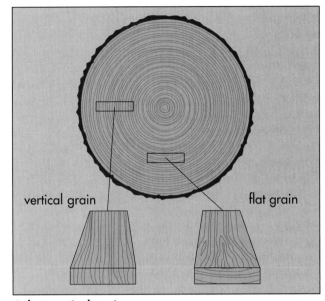

vertical grain   flat grain

Select vertical grains.

Depending on how the board was cut from the log, it may have vertical grain, with narrow grain lines running along the length of the board, or flat grain, with wider lines that sometimes form V-shapes. Many boards are a combination of the two. Choose boards that primarily are vertical grain. These are stronger, less likely to shrink and warp, and better looking.

WOOD SELECTOR

SPECIES	CHARACTERISTICS	COMMON EXTERIOR USES
Redwood	Durable and resistant to rot and insects if you get the darker-colored heartwood. Light and soft wood is not as strong as fir or Southern pine, but strong enough for some structural duties; easy to cut and sand.	Posts, beams, decking, fences, lattice, siding.
Cedar, cypress	Similar to redwood, the darker wood is rot resistant. Can be brittle; resists warping; pleasant aroma; easy to cut.	Siding, roof shakes and shingles, decking, rough trim.
Fir, larch	Heavy, very strong, and hard; holds nails well; good resistance to warping and shrinkage; a bit difficult to cut. The best wood for structural work; but because it is not porous, it has ugly incision marks when pressure-treated.	When treated, use for joists, beams, posts.
Hem/fir	A general classification that takes in a variety of species. Usually lightweight, soft, fairly strong; warps easily; may shrink; easy to cut.	When treated, use for joists, beams, posts.
Pine	Soft, light, fairly weak; good resistance to warping, but with a tendency to shrink; easy to cut.	Trim work if it will get painted or treated thoroughly.
Southern pine	Hard, stiff, excellent strength; holds nails well; has a tendency to crack, splinter, and warp. Often available as pressure-treated wood because it accepts the preservative easily and without incision marks.	When treated, use for joists, beams, decking, posts.
Spruce	Lightweight, soft, fairly strong; somewhat resistant to rot; resistant to splitting and warping; easy to work.	Fencing, framing.

MEASURING AND MARKING

Accurate measuring and marking are fundamental to successful carpentry. Though it may seem simple, a good measuring technique does not come naturally. It is a habit that takes practice to acquire. Don't rush when measuring; it is always worth your time to double-check. Adopt the carpenter's maxim, "Measure twice, cut once."

Get acquainted with your tape measure. Many a board has met its ruin because someone mistook a ¼-inch mark for a ⅛-inch mark. After measuring, always jot the figure on a piece of paper or a scrap of wood.

Mark carefully and clearly, using a sharp No. 2 pencil, the thin edge of a sharpened carpenter's pencil, or the blade of a utility knife.

Keep in mind that measuring tools can vary. If you and a co-worker are using different measuring tools, check that they both give the same reading.

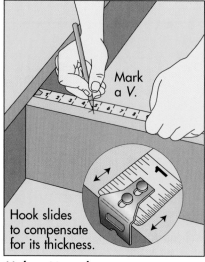

Make a V mark.
If you mark with a straight line, it will be easy to forget which end of the line marks the exact spot. A V mark shows you the exact spot. The hook at the end of the tape measure slides back and forth slightly, so you get an accurate measurement whether you hook it on the end of a board or push it against a surface.

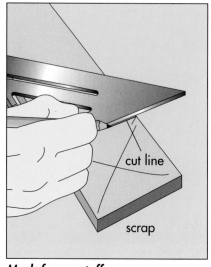

Mark for a cutoff.
For pinpoint accuracy, place the point of your pencil at the tip of the V, slide the square to it, and mark the cut line. The saw blade will cut out about ⅛ inch of the board, so make sure you cut on the correct side of the line. Drawing an X on the scrap side will eliminate confusion.

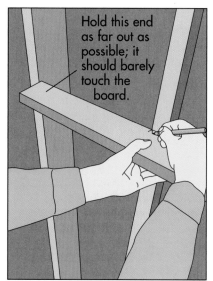

Hold in place and mark.
Usually the most accurate way to measure is to hold a piece where it needs to fit and mark it. First check one end for square, and butt it against one side of the opening. Hold the piece level and mark it with a V.

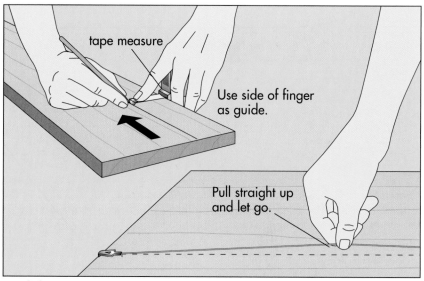

Mark for rip cuts.
If the line is parallel to the edge of the board and accuracy isn't critical, use your tape measure as a scribing device. Hold the tape so that a pencil laid against its end will make the correct line. Hold the tape and pencil firmly and pull toward you evenly, letting the tape body or your thumbnail slide along the board edge. For greater accuracy, make a V mark at both ends of the plywood or board and snap a chalk line between the marks. Or clamp a straightedge in place and draw a line.

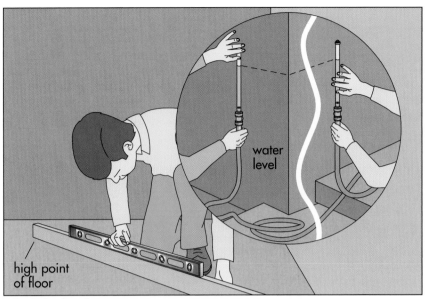

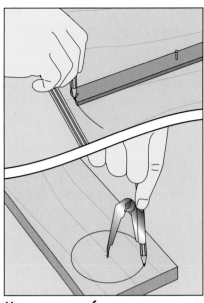

Check for level.

If possible, use a carpenter's level, or a level set on top of a straight board. If the points are far apart, use a water level. It works on the principle that water seeks its own level. A less expensive, but less reliable, option is a line level that hangs on a taut string. Test it for accuracy by turning it around— it should give the same reading both ways.

Use a compass for curves.

For wide circles, make a compass out of scrap wood. A notch holds the pencil in place for a smooth, accurate line. Use a metal compass for small circles.

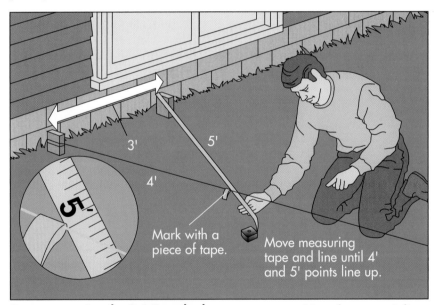

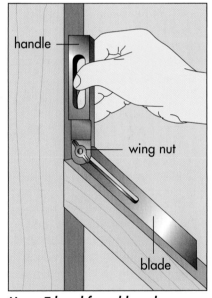

Square up using the 3-4-5 method.

To make sure the layout is square, start from a fixed point (a stake or a clear pencil mark) at one corner. Measure 3 feet along one side of your project site and pound in a stake or make a mark. Tie a mason's line to the first stake, stretch it beyond the proposed corner of your project, and attach it to another stake. Use a framing square to position the mason's line perpendicular to the face of the structure and tap the stake in place. Measure 4 feet along the second line and mark with a piece of tape; if the corner is square, the diagonal distance between those two points will equal 5 feet. If you are checking a large project for square, use multiples of 3, 4, 5; 6, 8, 10; or 9, 12, 15.

Use a T-bevel for odd angles.

If you want to duplicate an angle that is neither 45 nor 90 degrees, use a sliding T-bevel. Loosen the wing nut; push the tool in place until the handle rests against one edge and the blade against the other edge. Tighten the nut firmly, and take care not to bump the tool as you use it to make the duplicate mark where needed.

CUTTING WITH A CIRCULAR SAW

Chances are you will do most of your cutting on the outdoor project of your choice with a circular saw. Whether crosscutting 1-inch stock, ripping plywood, or trimming posts, you'll do the job better and more safely if you follow a few basic rules when using this versatile tool.

Whenever you cut, allow the saw to reach full operating speed, then slowly push the blade into the wood. Some carpenters look at the blade as they cut; others rely on the gunsight notch. Choose the method that suits you best. Avoid making slight turns as you cut. Instead, find the right path, and push the saw through the material smoothly. It will take some practice before you can do this consistently. This is a powerful tool with sharp teeth, so take care. It demands your respect.

CAUTION!
AVOID KICKBACK

It happens to even the most experienced carpenter: A blade binds, causing a circular saw to jump backward. Here is how to avoid this dangerous situation:
■ Support your work so the scrap won't bind the blade. Stabilize your work, especially with plywood, so the scrap remains stable.
■ Keep your blade sharp. Change it if you have to push hard to make it work.
■ Don't back up or try to make a turn when cutting. If your cut is going off line, stop the saw, back up, and start the cut again.
■ Be alert: Certain types of wood grain will grab the blade and cause it to kick back. Moist wood is also likely to grab the blade.

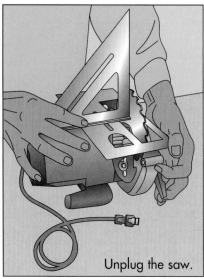

Unplug the saw.

Square the blade.
If the blade is not square, you will get inaccurate cuts. Hold a speed square against the blade (between the teeth) and adjust it. To test, crosscut a piece of 2x lumber. Flip the piece over and press cut edge against cut edge. If you see a gap at the top or bottom, the blade is not square.

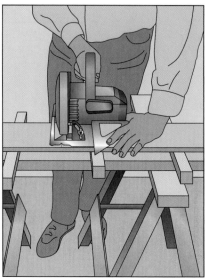

Support the material properly.
This is extremely important to ensure clean, safe cuts. If the scrap piece is short, support the board on the nonscrap side. If the scrap is long, it could bind the blade or splinter as it falls away at the end of the cut. To avoid this, support the lumber in four places.

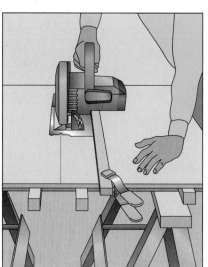

Use a guide for cutting plywood.
Chalk a line, begin cutting, and stop the blade without removing the saw. Clamp a straight piece of lumber in place against the blade guard; make sure it is the same distance from the chalk line on both ends. Complete the cut, using the straightedge as a guide.

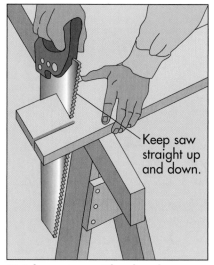

Keep saw straight up and down.

Finish a cutout with a handsaw.
To finish a notch, hold the handsaw so the blade is perpendicular to the work as you near the end of the cut. That way, the bottom of the board is cut the same distance as the top. Usually, it helps to reverse the position of the saw, as shown.

FASTENING WITH NAILS

The quickest way to make a job look unprofessional is to make a nailing mistake that mars the wood. All your careful measuring and cutting will be for naught if the wood ends up with smiles and frowns made by a hammer that missed the nail or if you bend a nail while driving it.

With practice, you'll be able to pound a nail home with smooth, fluid motions. Practice on scrap pieces before you pound nails into finished work. The longer and thicker the nail, the better it will hold. When possible, use the rule of three: A nail should be three times as long as the thickness of the board being fastened. If the nail heads will be exposed to moisture, choose galvanized nails to prevent rust. Special nails, such as ring shank, drive screw, and decking nails, hold better than standard ones. A headed nail holds better than a finish or casing nail.

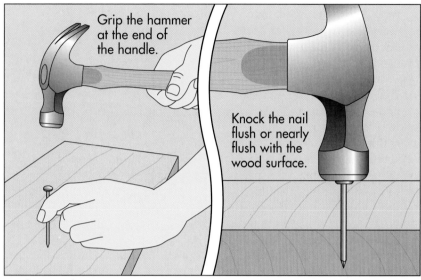

Nail properly.
Grasp the nail near its head and hold the hammer near the end of the handle. Lightly tap the nail until it stands by itself. Remove your hand. Keep your eye on the nail as you swing the hammer, letting the weight of the hammer head do the driving. To avoid a sore arm, swing from the shoulder, not the elbow. Your whole arm should move as you swing from the shoulder. Keep your wrist loose so you can give the hammer a final snap at the end of each blow. The entire motion should be relaxed and smooth. As you finish pounding, give the nail head a couple of gentler hits so it is nearly flush with the surface of the wood.

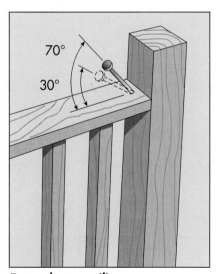

Fasten by toenailing.
Often, the only way to connect two boards is to drive nails at an angle. Position a nail 1 to 2 inches from the end of the board being fastened. Start pounding in the nail at about a 70-degree angle, then adjust it to about 30 degrees. Finish driving with a nail set.

Drill pilot holes.
If a nail splits the wood, it loses its holding power. Drill pilot holes before driving nails near the ends of boards or wherever the wood seems likely to crack. Use a drill bit that is slightly thinner in diameter than the nail you will be driving.

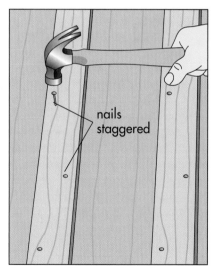

Stagger nails to avoid splits.
When driving nails along the length of a board, stagger them so you won't split the board. Avoid pounding neighboring nails through the same grain line; two nails will stress the grain twice as much as one. Where looks count, place nails in a regular pattern.

FASTENING WITH SCREWS AND BOLTS

Screws and bolts take a bit more time to install, but they fasten more tightly than nails; the threads of a screw grip wood fibers in a way that nails cannot. Bolts actually clamp adjoining members together. Screws and bolts have one additional advantage over nails: Often they can be removed without marring the job.

With a drill and a screwdriver bit you can drive screws almost as quickly as you can drive nails. A magnetic sleeve for the bit makes it easy to keep the screw in place as you work. As with nails, drill pilot holes wherever there is danger of splitting the wood.

When installing bolts, bore a hole that is only slightly larger that the thickness of the bolt you want to fasten. A socket wrench makes the work go quickly. Avoid overtightening, or you may damage the threads of the bolt.

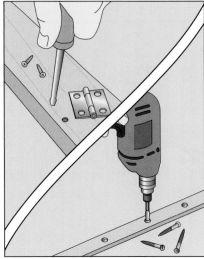

Make pilot holes, drive in screws.
Small screws can be fastened by first making a pilot hole with an awl, then driving the screw by hand. For larger screws, drill a pilot hole first. Drive Phillips-head or slotted screws with a variable-speed drill. Hold the sides of the head only, not the sharp threads; push firmly as you squeeze the trigger and drive the screw.

Use shields in a masonry surface.
The strongest way to attach a board to a brick or concrete wall is to use lag shields. Drill holes in the board, hold it in place, and mark for the holes in the wall. Remove the board, drill holes with a masonry bit, tap in the shields, and attach the board by driving lag screws into the shields using a socket wrench.

TOOLS TO USE

USE TWO DRILLS OR A KEYLESS CHUCK

If you need to drive several screws that need pilot holes, avoid changing the bit over and over again by using two drills, one with a boring bit and the other with a screwdriver bit. Or, use a drill with a keyless chuck, which makes quick work of changing bits.

FOR LARGE JOBS, USE A MAGNETIC SLEEVE

If you have many Phillips or slotted screws to install, consider buying a magnetic sleeve for your variable-speed drill. The sleeve fits in the chuck of the drill and holds the screw as you start it.

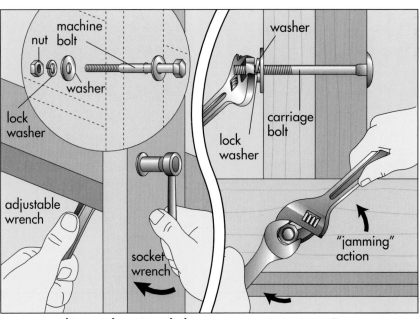

Secure machine and carriage bolts.
With machine bolts, use washers on both the head and the nut to keep them from biting into the wood. For extra hold, use a lock washer. Steady the nut with an adjustable wrench. Use a socket wrench to tighten the head.

Carriage bolts have flanges along their head that dig into the wood; use washers only on the threaded end. To keep a nut from working loose, thread another nut onto the bolt, snug against the first, then "jam" the two together by turning them in opposite directions.

INSTALLING POSTS AND FOUNDATIONS

Many outdoor projects call for installing posts. If the structure is attached to the house, or if it is fairly large, there is no need to sink the posts into the ground. You can rest them on top of footings, thereby ensuring against rot. But if the structure needs posts with lateral strength, you must set them in holes and then fill the holes with concrete, gravel, or tamped soil. Use pressure-treated posts with a preservative retention level of at least .40 (see page 10) or soak redwood or cedar in preservative.

When possible, set the posts in holes and build some of the structure before pouring concrete. That way, you can correct mistakes, and you will not be in danger of loosening the posts from their footings as you pound on them or lean ladders against them.

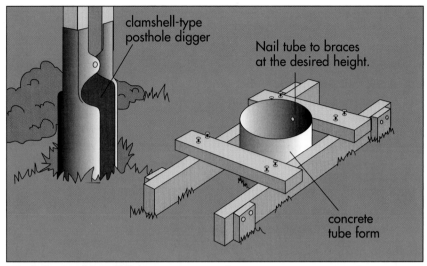

Dig holes and install forms.
A column form simply can be a long hole in the ground. To make the best use of concrete, try to be precise about your digging. Make the bottom of the hole a bit larger in diameter than the top to "key" it into the ground. Concrete tube

forms save on concrete because they are dimensioned precisely. If you want to continue the column footing above grade, brace the form. If you live in an area subject to freezing, you will need to dig below the frost line if you are building a major structure.

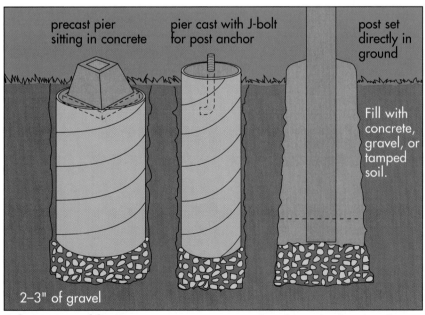

Select a type of footing.
Set a precast concrete pier into concrete. Choose one that is designed to hold a 4×4 post. For posts sunk in the ground, add a few inches of gravel to the bottom of the hole, so moisture can drain away from the post. When you fill the hole (with concrete, gravel, or

tamped soil), mound it up a bit above grade, so water will run away from the post. For posts that set atop a footing, sink a J-bolt in wet concrete and choose among several types of post anchors that attach to it. Some are adjustable so you can compensate for small mistakes (see page 9).

EXPERTS' INSIGHT

HELP WITH DIGGING POSTHOLES

■ Power augers should be handled by two people—even those designed for use by one person can wrench your back seriously if the blade runs into a rock or root. The easiest types of augers to handle are those mounted on a vehicle or those that are self-supporting (see page 8).

■ Fencing and landscaping contractors may have small, truck-mounted power augers for drilling holes. Save your back by hiring them to do it; the price may be reasonable. Be sure to have your holes clearly marked before the crew arrives.

APPLYING SEALERS AND FINISHES

On exterior projects, paint and stain are much more than a cosmetic: Often they are an important safeguard for keeping the wood from deteriorating. The final finish you apply to your outdoor project can help protect it from the three major enemies of exposed wood: sun, moisture, and wood-boring insects.

If the sun shines directly on unfinished wood, its ultraviolet (UV) rays will damage wood cells, but only to a depth of less than 1/32 inch. A cleaning or light sanding can restore the surface.

Moisture, sometimes in combination with direct sunlight, is the main cause of damage to wood. If wood goes through cycles of absorbing moisture and drying out, cupping, warping, and cracking can result. Once cracks appear, water seeps in deeper, accelerating damage. Also, moisture makes it easy for fungus and bacteria to grow, causing rot or mildew. Wood that stays wet for long periods of time inevitably will be damaged by rot.

If termites or other wood-boring insects are a problem in your area, expect them to attack your wood structures if they get a chance. Because such insects usually live in the ground and drill through the wood for food, most of the damage is not easily visible. Sealants and preservatives help discourage insect infestation.

Although using high-quality pressure-treated lumber or the heartwood of cedar or redwood is the best assurance that your project will last a long time, choosing the right finish and applying it correctly is an important second line of defense. Plan the finish at the same time as you plan the construction; it saves a lot of time and effort to stain or paint pieces before you put them together.

Seal and preserve your lumber.
It is important to keep moisture from soaking in, especially on boards with horizontal wooden surfaces. With a sealant, water will bead up and run off the wood.

Check your exterior wood surfaces periodically; you may need to apply preservative or sealer every year or so in high-wear areas and places exposed to exceptional moisture or sunlight.

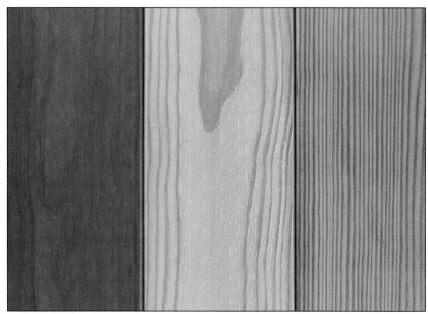

Select a stain.
Semiopaque and opaque stains (also called semitransparent and solid-color stains) are pigmented more heavily. A completely pigment-free, clear finish keeps moisture out but allows cedar or redwood to turn a silvery gray color. A product with ultraviolet (UV) inhibitors will prevent graying without changing the color, but it is expensive and short-lived. Semitransparent products often are the best choices—they prevent graying and have some pigment.

EXPERTS' INSIGHT

PROBLEMS THAT LOOK WORSE THAN THEY ARE

■ Gray stains on cedar or redwood are due to a mildew growing on the surface. If you don't like the look, clean it with a bleach solution, then stain.

■ Black stains on cedar usually result from a natural substance leaching out. Simply wash the wood with a mild soap solution.

■ Black mildew, caused by long-standing moisture, can be washed away with a bleach solution. To keep it from returning, take steps to allow the area to dry out. This may be as simple as sweeping away leaves and twigs regularly.

WHEN COLOR COUNTS

■ Green pressure-treated lumber has a color most people don't like. If left untreated it will turn a dingy gray. Brown-treated wood holds its color for several years before it needs restaining. To get the color you want, purchase stains specially formulated for pressure-treated lumber. Often, it makes sense to stain your material before building.

■ If you have old, stained wood, wash it with oxalic acid (wood bleach), household bleach, or a product made for this purpose. Brush it in well, rinse, and let the wood dry completely. Repeat if needed. Experiment on scraps until you get the color you like, then apply the stain.

■ Some wood contains natural agents that leach out over time, often from the knots, and cause stains to bleed through even several coats of paint. Pine and fir especially are prone to this problem. Also, older wood may have man-made stains that resist normal paints and finishes—and bleed through new finishes. The solution is to apply a stain-killing primer before painting. Of the many products available, the most effective are alcohol-based.

■ Primer assures that your paint will stick. If you are painting over old paint or if your surface is oily or grimy, there's a good chance that the new paint will start to peel within a year. To keep that from happening, clean the surface thoroughly and apply primer before painting.

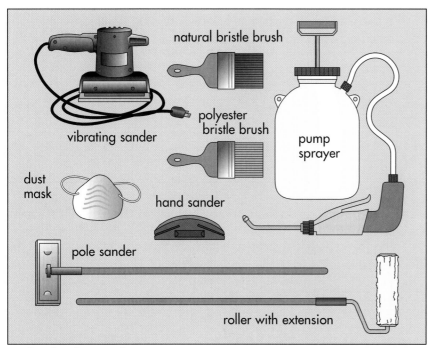

Gather finishing tools.
Use a **hand sander** for preparing wood for paint or stain; a **pole sander** if you have large surfaces to treat. To remove old stain or to prepare old and dirty wood, use a **vibrating sander**. Wear a **dust mask** when sanding. Use a natural bristle brush for oil-based finishes and a **polyester bristle brush** for water-based products. If you need to cover a large area with stain, have a helper apply the stain with a **roller** or a **pump sprayer** while you follow behind with a brush.

CAUTION!
USE SAFETY WHILE FINISHING WOOD

■ *Oil-soaked rags can burst into flames by themselves if they are piled up in a warm spot while damp. Air-dry your rags in the sun, then dispose of them or store them in an airtight container.*

■ *Take special care when sanding pressure-treated lumber. The copper arsenate is bonded tightly to the wood, making the lumber safe for normal uses. But sanding releases millions of tiny particles containing the toxic substance into the air. It won't do you serious harm, but it could make you sick. Wear a protective mask and always vacuum up all the dust when you're finished.*

DESIGNING FENCES AND GATES

Whether the fence you want to build is solely ornamental, purely functional, or a combination of the two, plan its style, scale, and finish to complement your home. Assess your home and lot carefully. Elaborate designs with an abundance of color look good standing alone but can overwhelm a simple house. Conversely, a simple fence style may not be appropriate for a home with elaborate architectural features. Bear function in mind as well: A lattice fence makes an adequate barrier for setting off a yard or garden, but you'll want sterner stuff for surrounding a pool or keeping a pet in the yard.

Gates, too, can vary in size and function. Some are intended only to mark entry into one area of the yard from another; others need to be built strong enough to be true barriers. And of course, fences and gates have their richest effect when combined with plantings.

ABOVE: *You can imitate the massive posts of this handsome fence by building a 1×8 box to surround each treated fence post. Set the box over the post and fasten it so it is 2 inches above the ground. Then cap each boxed post with a 2×10, capped in turn by a square of 1× wrapped with cove molding. Sturdy 2×2 pickets lend a touch of solid formality.*

LEFT: *In addition to their function as a doorway to an outdoor space, gates can be an attractive feature in their own right. Basic gate designs (see pages 28–31) are relatively simple to adapt to your choice of style and material. Most gates can be built and installed in a weekend.*

RIGHT: *Not every gate needs a fence; this gateway arbor transforms a simple gap in the hedge into an impressive outdoor entryway. Climbing plants and unfinished wood add a pleasant informality to the otherwise formal Palladian profile of the structure. To build a sandwiched-board gate like this, see page 31. Arbors adaptable to gates can be found on pages 34–37.*

BELOW: *This fence combines stately vertical-and-horizontal lattice sections with round cutouts, massive posts, and decorative post caps and newels. The 1×2 lattice provides better-than-average strength. Best of all, it sustains views while acting as a functional barrier.*

CUSTOMIZING PANELIZED FENCE SECTIONS

At your local building center, you can find premade fence sections that often cost less than if you bought the lumber and made the fence piece by piece. With a wide variety of patterns to choose from and a few slight changes to some of the pickets, you can easily and economically make a customized fence. If possible, customize the sections first, then install posts (see page 25). If your posts are already in place, you may have to adjust the width of the panels to fit the space.

YOU'LL NEED

TIME: 1 or 2 hours to modify a fence section.
SKILLS: Basic cutting, measuring, and fastening.
TOOLS: Nail puller, flat pry bar, drill, circular saw or sabersaw, hammer.

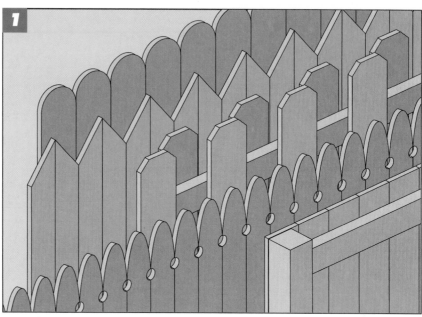

1. Select your panels.
Be sure the wood is rot resistant or plan on some heavy-duty painting. Check to see that the components are nailed together solidly. Don't accept panels that have cracked boards. You may need to add extra nails or screws to make a fence section strong. Make sure that the horizontal support pieces are placed where they will not get in the way of your planned modifications. Options shown above, top to bottom: scalloped, pointed, dog-eared, filigree, and straight.

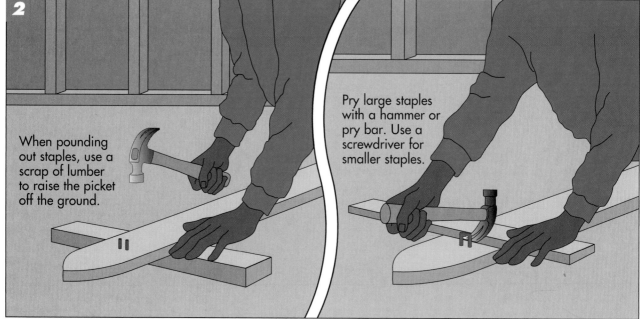

When pounding out staples, use a scrap of lumber to raise the picket off the ground.

Pry large staples with a hammer or pry bar. Use a screwdriver for smaller staples.

2. Remove pickets carefully.
Once you've decided on a pattern, you will need to remove some of the pickets to cut them or to move them. Experiment to find the best way to do this without marring the wood. Prying from behind with a claw hammer or a flat pry bar is often the best way. Or, pry out small staples with a screwdriver or pinchers (see page 26). When prying, use a scrap piece of wood to prevent the tool from damaging the pickets.

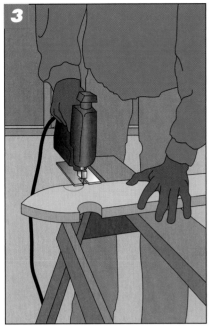

3. Cut a new picket design.

It may help to use a pencil compass to design a picket top. Experiment with scrap pieces that are the same width as your pickets. Once you have a design you like, use the board as a template for marking the others. Use a sabersaw to cut curved lines, or a circular saw for straight lines.

4. Reattach the modified pickets.

For the strongest joints, drill pilot holes and drive in decking screws. Choose fasteners that go most of the way through the picket and the framing piece but do not poke through them. You can make a pattern by varying the heights of the pickets. For a curved top line, remove all the pickets and put them back using a curved template (see below). Or vary the heights of the pickets according to a repeating pattern. In either case, make a chalk line cut at the bottom of the fence section after you reattach the pickets. Avoid nailing: It makes aligning pickets difficult, and can weaken the fence.

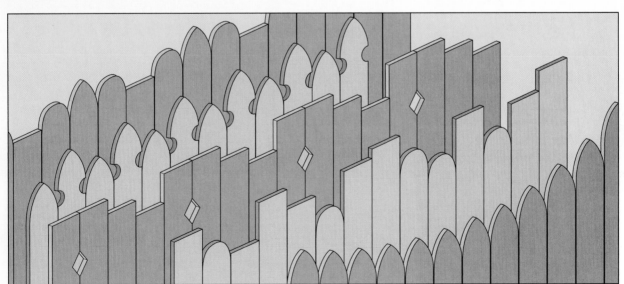

Mix and match pickets.

The design possibilities are endless. Use alternating picket tops either by removing and cutting every other picket or by purchasing panels with two types of pickets and mixing them together. Or install a taller, decorative picket every third or fourth one. You can make cutout peepholes, in diamond or other shapes, either by removing the pickets and cutting them or by cutting them with a sabersaw while the pickets are in place. For a unique look, arrange pickets at random heights, or mix picket-top designs.

INSTALLING A FENCED ENTRYWAY

Not only will a fenced entryway be an attractive addition to your home, it will keep bike riders and walkers from taking a shortcut across your lawn. In addition, it will create an ideal setting for ornamental plantings.

Most of the basic principles and techniques of building a fence are involved in this project. Fences have three basic components: Posts provide lateral strength, top and bottom rails span the distance between the posts, and pickets (or sometimes, latticework) attach to the rails. If you choose to add a gate, see pages 28–31.

Begin by checking local setback requirements. Then lay out the posthole locations using mason's lines and stakes to establish straight lines. Use the 3-4-5 method (see page 13) when you

need to establish a square corner.

Panelized sections of fencing are the easiest to work with. To ensure the distance between panels is correct, set one post, position the panel, and then set the second post (see page 26).

Apply extra preservative to the parts of the posts to be inserted into the ground. Shovel 2 to 3 inches of gravel into the bottom of each hole, set the post in, and plumb it in both directions. You may need to stake it in place temporarily. Install all the posts a little taller than they need to be so you can trim them to the correct height later. Fill the holes with tamped soil or concrete (allow the concrete to cure for a few days before proceeding).

If your yard is fairly level, you may want to cut all the posts at

the same level for a neat appearance. Use a line or water level to mark them. If you have a sloping yard, use a chalk line to mark for a straight slope, or just cut each post to the same height above grade; the fence sections will be at various heights. Cut each post by marking a line all the way around its perimeter with a square, then cutting with a circular saw.

YOU'LL NEED

TIME: With a helper, about a day.
SKILLS: Measuring and laying out, digging postholes, cutting, fastening, painting.
TOOLS: Posthole digger, mason's line and stakes, circular saw, handsaw, level, drill, hammer.

Build a picket entryway.
Build an entryway like this right next to the sidewalk, or set it back 2 to 3 feet to leave room for plantings. Though it is low and mostly decorative, it does need to be built strongly in case people lean or bump against it. If you have a corner lot, it may make sense to have one side longer than the other, but in most cases it will look best if it is symmetrical. The post caps and newels shown are just two examples of the many types available at lumberyards and home centers. For modified picket designs, see page 23.

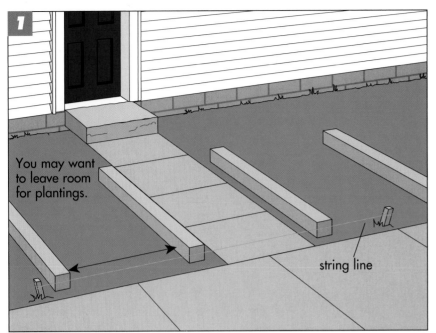

1. Lay out the posts.

Establish a straight line for your fence by pounding two small stakes into the ground beyond both ends of the fence. Choose the locations of your posts along the mason's line. For most designs, the posts should be no more than 6 feet apart.

When purchasing posts, take into account the depth of the hole (see Step 3) and make sure they are longer than they need to be—you will cut them to height later.

Prepare for digging the postholes by cutting out the sod so your auger won't go astray as you dig.

2. Dig the postholes.

Use a clamshell-type digger for a few easy holes or rent a power auger (the type shown here can be used by one person), or hire someone to dig the holes for you. For most situations, a hole that is 30 inches deep will give you enough strength.

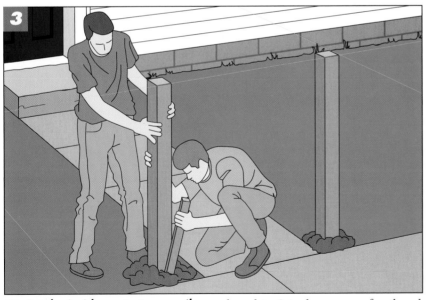

3. Set the inside posts, tamp soil.

Shovel a few inches of gravel into the bottom of each posthole; this will allow water to drain away from the post bottoms to prevent rot. Set the two inside posts in the holes. As your helper holds the post plumb in both directions,

shovel in 8 inches or so of soil and tamp it firm with a long 2×2 or a piece of metal reinforcing bar—do a thorough job. Repeat until the hole is filled and mounded up a bit to help water drain away from the post.

EXPERTS' INSIGHT

LONG-LASTING POSTS

Do things right to avoid having to replace posts in a few years. Select pressure-treated lumber with a preservative retention level of at least .40 or that has been treated for ground contact. Or get dark-colored heartwood of cedar or redwood, if possible, and thoroughly soak the ends in a sealer/preservative.

To really hold posts in place, set them in concrete rather than in tamped soil. Also, pound at least eight nails part way into the base of the post to ensure a tight bond between post and concrete.

4

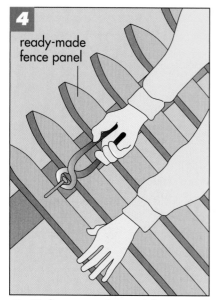

ready-made fence panel

5

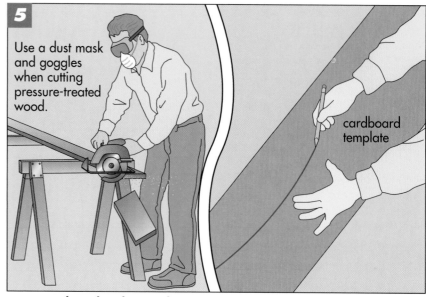

Use a dust mask and goggles when cutting pressure-treated wood.

cardboard template

4. Make or purchase pickets.

You can make pickets out of 1×
by cutting one picket to the design
of your choice and using it as a
template to cut others with a
sabersaw. Using pickets removed
from a ready-made fence panel
(see page 22) is a faster and more
economical method.

5. Cut rails and make template.

Have a helper hold the outside
posts plumb (you'll set them later),
while you measure for the length
of the top and bottom rails. Cut
the rails so they will fit between
the two posts. If you choose to
position the pickets so their tops
are arched rather than inclined, as

shown on page 27, make a
template. It must be as long as a
fence section and it should have
a smooth, sweeping arch. Cut it
wide enough so it can rest on the
top rail as you use it. Draw it
freehand, or use a compass made
of pencil and string, or a notched
piece of wood (see page 13).

6

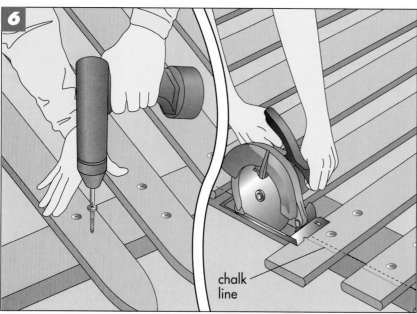

chalk line

7

Set outside post after section is positioned.

6. Fasten the pickets.

Lay the top and bottom rails on a
flat surface, such as a well-swept
garage floor. Measure to make
sure rails are the correct distance
apart on both ends and square to
each other. Use a board as a guide
for an inclined effect or a cardboard
template on the floor with its

bottom edge resting against the top
rail. Set the pickets on top of the
rails so their tops follow the guide.
Set them all out before fastening
so you can stand back and check
that you've achieved the desired
effect. Attach to the rails with nails
or screws. Make a chalkline cut at
the bottom.

7. Set the outside posts.

Put the fence section in place
against the inside post. Put
temporary blocks under it to hold
it off the ground at least an inch.
Have a helper hold it while you
set the outside post in the hole.
Adjust the post so it fits snugly
against both rails. Set the post.

EXPERTS' INSIGHT

NOTCHING FENCE RAILS INTO POSTS

Attaching the rails to your fence posts by toenailing will work in most circumstances, but if the fence is likely to be leaned on or in the path of prevailing winds, consider setting the rails in notches cut in the posts.

First determine the location of the rail. Use a square to draw a top cut line and a scrap of rail to strike a bottom cut line. (For a 2×4 rail, this would be 3½ inches.) Set your circular saw to a depth equal to the thickness of the rail (1½ inches for a 2×4). Make four or five cuts between the lines. Chisel out the excess and fasten the rail in place.

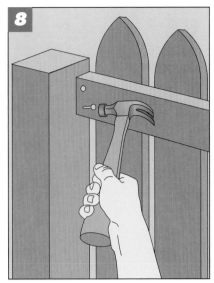

8. Attach the panel.
Hold the rails tightly against the post. Drill pilot holes to prevent splitting, and drive toenails or angled screws through the rails and into the post. Finish driving with a nail set to prevent marring the wood. For extra strength, add metal angle brackets or small wood cleats.

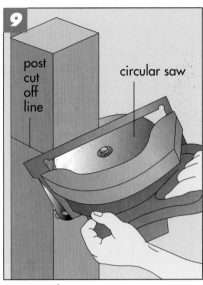

9. Trim the posts.
After you have attached both rail sections, mark the posts for cutting by using a square to mark a line on all four sides of the post. Set your circular saw to its full depth and make a cut, taking care not to damage the pickets. Finish the cut with a handsaw.

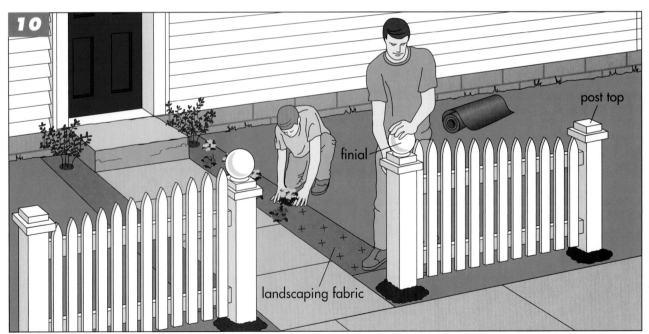

10. Add post caps, finials.
Post tops are not just decorative. If you simply leave the posts cut flat, rain water will seep into the wood through the end grain. Even high-quality pressure-treated lumber will develop cracks if the ends are exposed. You can make a post top by cutting a piece of 2×6 square to 5½ by 5½ inches. Chamfer the edges with a plane, circular saw, or belt sander. Attach the caps with casing nails, countersink the nails, and fill with caulk. Purchase manufactured finials at your home center or lumber yard. Bore holes and attach the finials using the double-threaded screws provided. Paint the fence with two coats of exterior paint or apply a generous coat of sealer with UV protection. Finally, complete your decorative plantings. Landscaping fabric covered with mulch limits weeds.

BUILDING A Z-FRAME GATE

This gate is sturdy and easy to make. The more closely spaced the pickets, the stronger the gate. You will probably want to use the same pickets on your gate as are on the fence. But don't be afraid to mix up designs a bit. A gate with a curved top adds visual interest to a straightforward fence.

Choose your hardware along with the gate design. Any of the three types shown on page 9 will work well; they simply attach to the post differently. A T-hinge is stronger than a strap hinge, but a screw-hook hinge is the strongest, and makes it easy to remove the gate—simply lift it up.

YOU'LL NEED

TIME: Half a day to build and hang a gate.
SKILLS: Measuring, checking for square, cutting, fastening with screws or nails.
TOOLS: Drill, framing square, circular saw, sabersaw, hammer.

EXPERTS' INSIGHT

WEIGHT VS. STRENGTH

A massive gate may be stronger in itself, but its extra weight requires heavy-duty hinges and may strain your posts. A lighter gate is easier to use, can be installed with lighter hardware, and looks less forbidding. Consider the use and abuse the gate will get. If kids will be hanging on it, you may want to build a stronger box-frame or sandwich gate. In addition, make sure the post is strong, and install heavy-duty hinges.

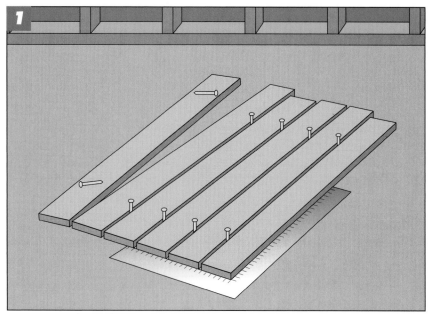

1. Lay out the pickets.
Cut the pickets roughly to length (you will cut the tops off later) and lay them on a well-swept, flat surface. Space them evenly apart, with at least ⅛-inch space between them so the wood can expand and contract. If possible, space them so they come out to the exact width you want. If not, cut the pieces on either side. Avoid narrow pieces. Use a framing square to make sure the bottom corners are square.

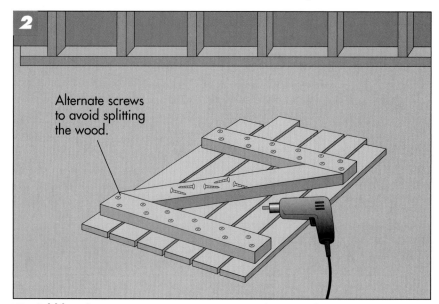

Alternate screws to avoid splitting the wood.

2. Add bracing.
Cut two 2×4s to the width of the gate, minus ¼ inch. Taking care not to bump the pickets out of alignment, set the 2×4s on top of the pickets parallel to each other and about 4 inches from the bottom and the top of the gate. At each joint, drive in two 2-inch decking screws. Drill pilot holes using an alternating pattern to avoid splitting the wood. Hold a 2×4 diagonally from the top of the hinge side to the bottom of the latch side and mark for cutting. Cut and install it in the same way.

half the width

Cut above, not through, the brace.

3. Mark a curve and cut.
Turn the gate over and place it on a set of horses or a table so you can cut it. Make a compass out of a pencil and string or use a notched strip of wood (page 13) to draw a curve on the top. Take care that the cut won't go below the top brace on the sides. Cut along your guideline with a sabersaw and lightly sand all the edges. Paint the gate or apply sealer. (See page 31 for how to hang the gate and install a latch.)

4. Prepare the posts.
Plumb and brace your posts carefully. If the hinge post is not plumb in both directions, the gate will either close or open by itself and you'll need to install a gate-closing spring. Firmly tamp soil around the base of each post or set the post in concrete.

Vary materials and finish.
A simple Z-frame gate suits a weathered picket fence (above) or a formal, crisply painted entryway (above right). Use stain or a sealer/preservative if you want the wood grain to shine through for a rustic look. Opaque stain has a subdued matte finish. Use an outdoor enamel for a shiny finish. If you paint, be sure to apply at least two coats; incompletely painted wood looks less finished than unpainted wood.

MAKING A BOX-FRAME GATE

This gate is a bit sturdier than a Z-frame and takes a good deal longer to build. But don't be afraid to tackle it if it is the look you want. This simple square or rectangular frame is braced by a diagnonal member. The tricky part is the half-lap joint. A tablesaw or radial-arm saw will make this easier, but you can make a good-looking joint with a circular saw if you work carefully. As with all gates, start by making sure your opening is flanked by two firmly set and plumb posts (see page 29).

YOU'LL NEED

TIME: Most of a day to build and hang a gate.
SKILLS: Measuring and squaring, cutting, making a half-lap joint, fastening with nails or screws.
TOOLS: Circular, table-, or radial-arm saw; drill; hammer; carpenter's square; tape measure.

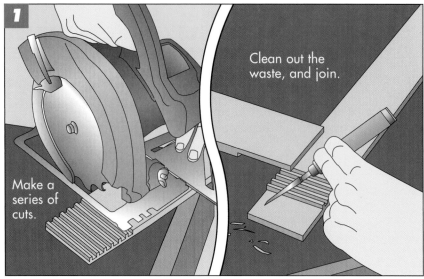

Make a series of cuts.

Clean out the waste, and join.

1. Make a frame with lap joints.
Cut the frame pieces. Set your saw to cut to a depth exactly one-half the thickness of the framing pieces. Experiment with scrap pieces to make sure this is precise. Hold one board on top of the other to mark for the joints. Cut to the inside of the line; make a series of closely spaced cuts in the area of the joint. Chisel out the remaining wood. Cut the other piece the same way. Dry-fit to make sure the pieces fit tightly. Apply exterior carpenter's glue, clamp, drill pilot holes, and drive two 1¼-inch screws. Check for square as you work.

2. Brace the frame.
Hold a piece of 2×4 in place, running diagonally, and mark for cutting. After cutting carefully, set it inside and fasten it to the frame by drilling pilot holes and driving 3-inch screws. The tighter this joint, the stronger the gate.

Use an alternating pattern to avoid splits.

3. Attach pickets and hardware.
Evenly space the pickets on the frame, or plan to cut the outside pickets a bit—avoid narrow pieces on the sides. Attach to the frame by drilling pilot holes and driving 2-inch screws, taking care that they don't poke through. See page 31 for how to hang the gate.

Williamsburg-style closer
Here's a disarmingly simple closing mechanism. Install a short post near the hinge post of the gate, attach a chain to both posts, and add a weight to the chain. The classic design uses a cannonball but you can use any object weighing 5 pounds or so—the heavier the weight, the more firmly the gate will close. Kits include faux cannonballs.

BUILDING A SANDWICHED GATE

Because the solid boards on this gate are placed diagonally, they help brace the gate. For the strongest design, use tongue-and-groove boards, but regular 1× pieces with spaces between them work well. With a sandwich design, the gate will look the same from both sides. You may want to place a 2×3 or 2×4 cap on top of the gate for protection against rainwater. If not, apply plenty of sealer or paint to the exposed end grain on top. Prepare a working area for this project by sweeping debris from a driveway or walk.

YOU'LL NEED

TIME: About a half day to build and hang the gate.
SKILLS: Measuring and squaring, cutting, driving screws or nails.
TOOLS: Drill, carpenter's square, circular saw, chalk line.

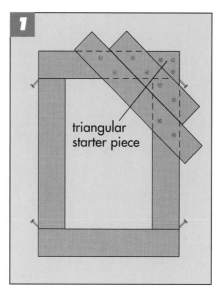

1. Build a frame and lay out.
Lay out one set of 1×6 frame pieces. Nail or screw them together so they won't come apart as you work. Set the diagonals on the frame starting with a 45-degree-cut triangle in the corner, and allowing the other pieces to hang over the edge. Drill pilot holes and drive 1¼-inch screws for all joints.

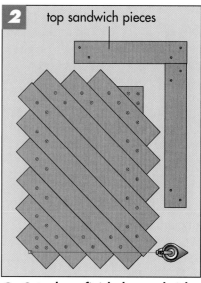

2. Cut edges, finish the sandwich.
Drill pilot holes and use an alternating pattern for the screws, to avoid splitting boards. Chalk lines for all four edges. Set the circular saw blade so it barely cuts through the diagonals (not the frame), and cut carefully. Add the top sandwich pieces, drilling pilot holes and driving 2-inch screws.

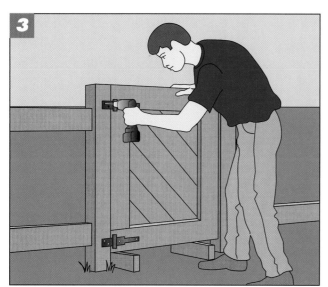

3. Hinge the gate.
Set the gate on blocks so the top of the gate lines up with the top of the fence post and the side is flush against the post. For a strap or T-hinge, hold the hinge in place, drill pilot holes, and drive the screws. For a screw-hook hinge, drill a pilot hole at a 45-degree angle into the post, screw in the hook, slip on the hinge strap, and fasten it to the gate.

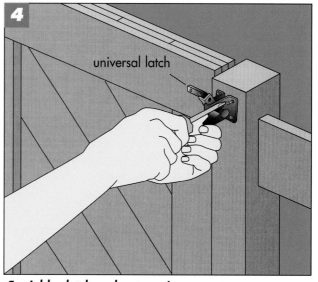

4. Add a latch and gate spring.
A universal latch clicks shut automatically. Put the gate in its fully closed position and attach the pieces with screws. If the gate needs to be openable from the outside, drill a hole and run a string through it. Install a gate spring if you want the gate to close automatically.

DESIGNING ARBORS AND TRELLISES

The filtered light and graceful lines of these structures, often softened by climbing plants, add a touch of relaxed elegance to any yard. Choose the stately, crisp lines of smooth, painted lattice pieces, or go with the rustic charm of stained rough wood. Lattice sections can cover up unsightly areas or provide privacy without seeming unfriendly. Though you may choose to hire a pro, many of these structures are easier to build than you might think. A rich ornamental look can be achieved simply by laying several kinds of materials on top of each other. And premade lattice panels can be purchased and easily installed— add some trim, and they will look custom-made.

RIGHT. *A simple overhead structure is made from cut logs nailed or lashed together with copper wire.*

BELOW. *This arbor uses repeating curved cuts on standard-dimensional lumber to make a rich custom look.*

ABOVE. *This elegant overhead transforms a small patio into an attractive outdoor room. A trellis preserves privacy. The alternating pattern of the pickets on the trellis makes it more ornate-looking. Here, two different lengths of pickets in a repeating pattern create open viewing areas. The winglike rafters on the overhead structure can be designed easily and cut with a circular saw.*

RIGHT. *An arched arbor makes a beautiful entranceway in a fence as well as providing a place for plants to climb. The arches require some skill and extra tools to build (see pages 36–37), but are well within the range of most do-it-yourselfers. The posts and lattice work (see pages 42-44) are easy to install. An arched arbor with seats makes a delightful garden retreat.*

BUILDING A BASIC ARBOR

This design has a solid look and feel with a touch of whimsy on the top. Designing and cutting the wing-like joists will be challenging, but can be fun as well. Install 6×6 posts for a massive look, or use 4×4s to save money and make the structure look lighter. A suggested size for the arbor is 4 feet by 4 feet. Use rot-resistant lumber (see pages 10–11). Set the posts in concrete and wait a few days before completing the arbor. Or build the entire structure and pour the concrete afterwards.

YOU'LL NEED

TIME: Two days, plus time for the concrete to cure.
SKILLS: Basic carpentry.
TOOLS: Posthole digger, circular saw, high-quality sabersaw, handsaw, level, drill.

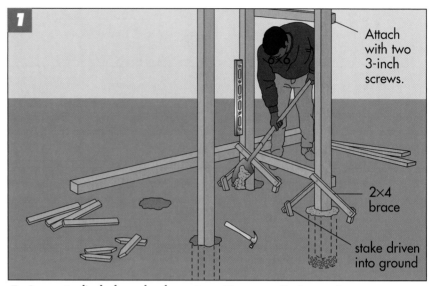

Attach with two 3-inch screws.

2×4 brace

stake driven into ground

1. Lay out, dig holes, plumb posts.
Lay the arbor out, using the 3-4-5 method to make sure it is square (see page 13). Dig postholes at least 30 inches deep, shovel in 3 inches of gravel, and set in the posts. Cut four 2×4 braces to the desired width of the arbor and attach them to the posts as shown.

Temporarily brace the posts so they are plumb in both directions. Check again for square; try to be within a half inch of perfection. Shovel in concrete to fill the hole, mounding it up a bit at the top so water will run away from the posts. Or tamp soil firmly into the hole.

Cut line is level with the other 3 posts.

2. Cut the post tops.
Cut all the posts level with each other 9 feet above the ground. Use a level sitting on top of a straight board to mark for this. To cut a 6×6, cut all four sides with a circular saw, and finish cutting the middle with a handsaw.

lattice panel

1×2 nailer

3. Attach lattice and nailers.
For each side, cut a lattice panel so it slightly overhangs the 2×4 braces evenly on bottom and top, and attach it with 1¼-inch screws. On the inside of the arbor, attach 1×2 nailers and screw the lattice to the nailers.

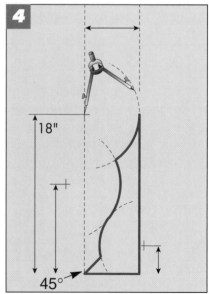

18"

45°

4. Make a template for the rafters.
On a piece of cardboard, draw a rectangle 5½ inches wide and about 18 inches long to represent the end of a 2×6 rafter. With a compass, draw arcs as shown or make up your own design. Cut out the template with a utility knife.

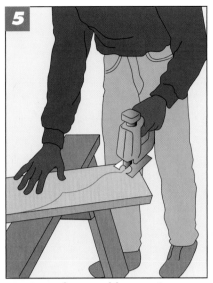

5. Cut rafters and beam pieces.

Cut 2×6s to the length you want for rafters and beam pieces—about 30 inches longer than the width or length of the arbor. Mark the ends with the template and cut. Cutting is easy using a high-quality sabersaw. Consider renting a professional model for this job to ensure you get good, clean cuts.

6. Attach beams and rafters.

To make the beams, attach four pieces, one on each side of the posts, their tops flush with the tops of the posts, and attach using 3-inch deck screws. Wrap posts with 1×2 trim; drill pilot holes for 6d casing nails. Space the rafters evenly, and attach by angle-driving 3-inch deck screws.

7. Add the top pieces.

Lay out for regularly spaced 1×2 top pieces. These are not just for appearances; they keep the rafters from warping. Attach them by drilling pilot holes and driving 1⅝-inch deck screws.

Finish the structure by giving it a couple of good coats of paint or sealer/preservative.

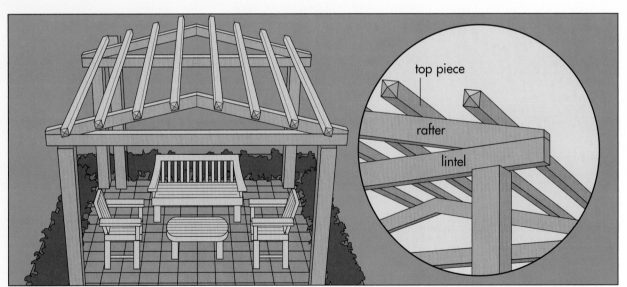

Variation: peaked arbor.

If you want a larger width or a different look, consider a peaked arbor. Install the posts and, if desired, the lattice sections as you would for the square arbor. For the lintel and rafters, use 4×6s as shown for a very solid look, or use 2×6s.

Cut the lintel 3 inches longer than the opening. With a helper, lift it into place on top of the posts, so it overhangs each post 1½ inches on each side and is flush in front. To determine the angles for the cuts on the rafters, have a couple of helpers hold pieces in place while you mark.

All four rafter pieces must be identical. Install them with 3-inch deck screws. Working carefully because the rafters will be unstable, add the top pieces—either 4×4s or 2×4s—by drilling pilot holes and angle-driving 3-inch screws.

BUILDING AN ARCHED ARBOR

Do-it-yourselfers often are leery of building curved structures. But you can build this one if you have basic skills and some patience. For the arbor, use rot-resistant lumber, and choose 1×8s that have no large knots for the arch pieces.

This arbor has a simple lattice made of horizontal 1×3s. The arched top supplies the visual interest. If you want further variation, simply add vertical 1×3s, evenly spaced, about 6 feet tall on either side.

YOU'LL NEED

TIME: Two days to build the arbor and finish it.
SKILLS: Basic carpentry, cutting curves with a sabersaw.
TOOLS: Posthole digger, level, circular saw, drill, sabersaw, and 9 or 10 clamps.

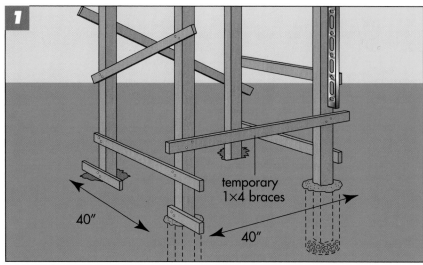

1. Set the posts in concrete.

Mark the ground for four posts square to each other. A recommended size is 40 inches square. Dig holes, 30 inches deep or more, and shovel in 3 inches or more of gravel. Temporarily brace the posts so they are plumb in both directions. Recheck for square. You can pour the concrete now and wait for a few days for it to cure before building the arbor; or firmly brace temporarily, build the arbor, and pour the concrete at the end of the job. Or shovel in soil and firmly tamp it down. Make sure the concrete or tamped soil is mounded up so water will run away from the posts.

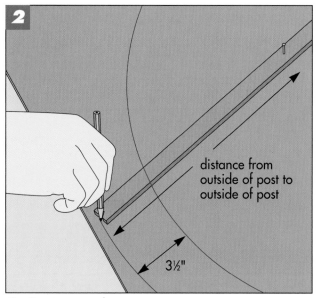

2. Draw a template.

Measure the distances between posts to make sure you have the exact dimension that your arches must span (outside to outside). On a large piece of cardboard or paper, make a pattern for your arches, using a notched-wood compass (see page 13). The arch will form exactly half of a circle, and will be 3½ inches wide. Cut out the template.

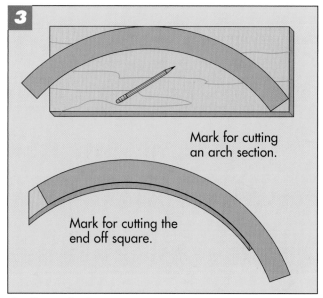

Mark for cutting an arch section.

Mark for cutting the end off square.

3. Cut arch pieces.

Cut the template in half to make it easier to use. Cut the ends square. Lay the template on pieces of 1×8 and mark for 12 curved pieces, all of them as long as possible. Cut out the pieces with a jigsaw, working carefully for smooth cuts. Don't worry about making all the pieces the same length; you will cut them off later.

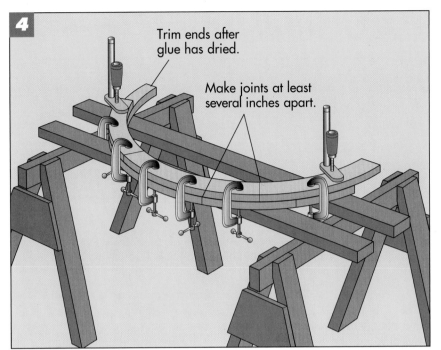

Trim ends after glue has dried.

Make joints at least several inches apart.

4. Laminate and trim the arches.

You will use six pieces for each arch. Lay them out so that the joints are offset, as shown; if the joint of a top piece is within 2 inches of a bottom joint, the arch will be weakened. Apply squiggles of a strong glue to one full arch and clamp the pieces together as shown. Allow the glue to dry completely.

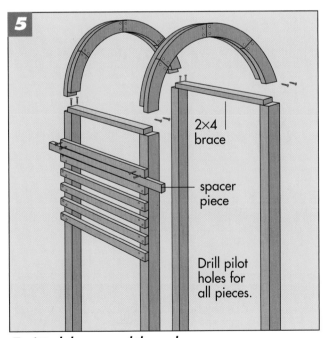

2×4 brace

spacer piece

Drill pilot holes for all pieces.

5. Attach braces and the arch.

Using 3-inch deck screws, attach two 2×4 horizontal braces to the top of the posts, leaving 1½ inches of space at each end for the inner arch pieces. With a helper, set the arches in place and attach them to the braces, drilling pilot holes and driving 3-inch screws. The arches will be wobbly so work carefully.

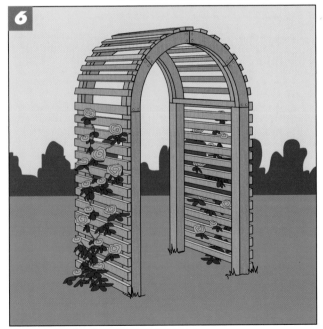

6. Attach the lattice pieces.

Use a spacer piece (step 5) to make sure all the lattice pieces form a regular pattern. Drill pilot holes for all the screws. As you add the top pieces, you will feel the arch growing more stable. Paint the structure or apply stain and sealer. Because plants will grow on it, it is important to apply plenty of finish—it will be hard to reapply later.

ADDING AN ATTACHED SUNSHADE

Adding a sunshade that attaches to your house offers advantages over building a freestanding structure. The ledger provides a solid starting point, reducing wobble while you're building, and it eliminates two posts, making the space underneath more open.

To prevent wood warping and materials pulling apart over time, be sure to use the right-sized lumber and to fasten it securely. Use lumber that is rot resistant.

YOU'LL NEED

TIME: Two days with a helper for a sunshade like the one shown.
SKILLS: Basic carpentry skills.
TOOLS: Ladders, circular saw, drill, sabersaw, hammer, level, chalk line, tape measure.

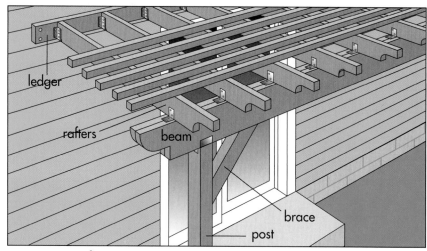

Putting it together.
For the ledger and the rafters, use 2×6 boards for spans up to 12 feet, 2×8s for spans up to 16 feet, and 2×10s for spans up to 20 feet. This assumes only light materials sitting on top of the rafters; if you will be adding significant weight, you'll need sturdier rafters. Local codes also may call for different dimensions.

The top pieces are important not only for creating shade, but also to keep the rafters from warping. You may want to change the configuration depending on which direction the sunshade is facing and how much shade you want.

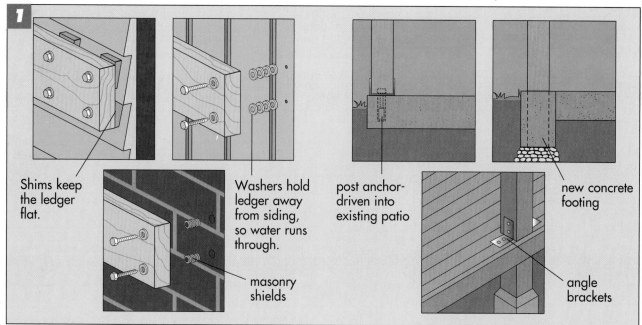

Shims keep the ledger flat.

Washers hold ledger away from siding, so water runs through.

masonry shields

post anchor-driven into existing patio

new concrete footing

angle brackets

1. Install ledger and anchor posts.
Cut a ledger board to the length of your sunshade and attach it firmly to your house, making sure it is level. For a frame house, attach to the studs or to the floor framing for the second story. Use shims to make the ledger sit flat and then flash or caulk the top. Or use washers to hold the ledger away from the house so water can run through and the wood can dry out. To attach to a masonry wall, use masonry screws or shields as shown (see page 16).

Cut the posts longer than they need to be. On a patio surface, use a post anchor, or dig a posthole and set the post in concrete. If the posts will rest on a deck, crawl under the deck (if possible) and drive screws up into the posts. Otherwise, use angle brackets.

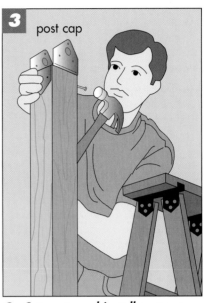

width of the beam

post cap

2. Plumb posts, mark for cutting.

Temporarily brace the posts so they will be firm while you work on them. Check the posts for plumb in both directions.

The beam will rest on top of the posts, so you will cut them as high as the bottom of the ledger, minus the width of the beam. With a helper, use a level sitting atop a straight board or a line level to mark the corner post for cutting to exact height. If you will have an interior (noncorner) post, run a tight chalkline from corner post to corner post to mark for cutting it.

Another option: Cut the post to the height of the bottom of the ledger, and make a beam by attaching boards on either side of the posts, flush to the top of the post (see page 34).

3. Cut posts and install post caps.

Draw a line all the way around each post using a square, and cut two sides with a circular saw. Attach a post cap on top.

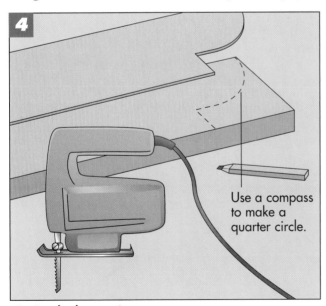

Use a compass to make a quarter circle.

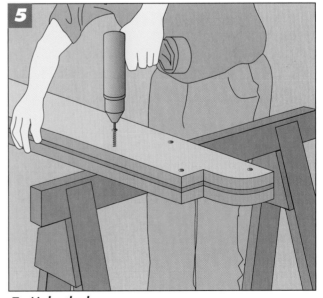

4. Cut the beam pieces.

Make a template for the beam and rafter ends on a piece of cardboard that is the same width as the lumber. Use the scallop design shown above, or make up your own (see page 34). Cut the first beam piece to length (remember, it will overhang the posts), and then cut out the decorative ends on both sides with a sabersaw. Use it as a template for the other piece.

5. Make the beam.

Cut pieces of ½-inch pressure-treated plywood into strips the same width as the beam pieces. Sandwich the boards together, and fasten them with 3-inch deck screws driven in an alternating pattern every 4 to 6 inches. This will make a very strong beam that is 3½ inches thick—just right for placing on top of a 4×4 post.

6. Attach and brace the beam.

With a helper, set the beam into the post caps, making sure it overhangs the posts the same length on both sides. Drive 1¼-inch screws or 6d galvanized nails to hold the beam in place.

To make a brace, cut a 4×4 at a 45-degree angle on both sides. Check your circular saw to make sure its blade is square (see page 14). Mark for the cut as shown, and cut the two angle-marked sides. To install the brace, have a helper hold it in place, so both ends are tight and flush to the beam and the post. Drill pilot holes and drive two 3-inch screws at each joint.

7. Cut the rafters.

Cut a rafter to length, taking into account the overhang. The design shown above is the reverse of the beam design; use the template that you used for the beam, and hold it backwards. Cut both ends of one rafter, and use it as a template for the others.

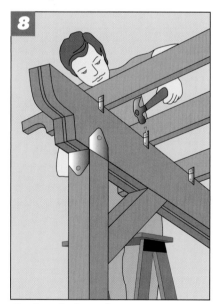

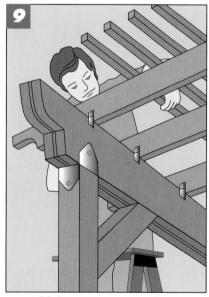

8. Attach the rafters.

Lay out the rafters first so they will be evenly spaced. For extra strength, use hurricane ties as shown. Or, drill pilot holes and angle-drive deck screws if you don't like the look of the ties.

9. Add the top pieces.

Cut the 2×2 top pieces to length. Experiment with different spacings, to see how much shade you want. One attractive option is to "self-space," that is, to use a scrap piece of 2×2 as a spacer. Attach to the rafters by driving a 3-inch decking screw at each joint.

EXPERTS' INSIGHT

OTHER CANOPY MATERIALS

For a richly textured look, install several layers of criss-crossed materials on top; for instance, a layer of 1×2s on top of the 2×2s in this design.

Other canopy options include rolls of reed, bamboo, and shade cloth. If winters are harsh where you live, store your canopy during winter to prolong its life. Ready-made sheets of lattice can work, but use a heavy-duty material that is a full ¾-inch thick, and support it every 12 inches.

For protection against rain, the roof must slope away from the house at least ½ inch per running foot. Install stretched canvas or corrugated fiberglass panels on top.

PLANNING AN OUTDOOR ROOM

By combining several of the projects described in this book, you can create an outdoor living area that has the feeling of an enclosed space while preserving the pleasure of being outdoors. Often you can transform an area marred by street noise or an unpleasant view into an enjoyable outdoor room.

The base for the room can be a deck or patio—any smooth surface suitable for outdoor furniture. If you need a new surface, prefab modular wooden squares are the quickest to install, followed by pavers or flagstones set in a bed of sand. You'll also want to install a permanent flagstone or paver walkway to the room.

Once you've settled on the location of your outdoor room, decide how much privacy and wind or sound buffering you want. Often installing a grillwork screen (see pages 42–43), fence (see pages 22–23), or a dense hedge on one or two sides will provide the needed protection. For the side facing your house, a bench, planters, or a flower bed can clearly mark the boundaries of the room without limiting access.

Too much sun can be more bane than blessing. The best solution may be to cover the southern half of the room with an overhead structure (see pages 38–40) so that about two-thirds

of the area will be shaded. Space the overhead rafters to produce more or less filtered light depending on your climate and the number of nearby shade trees in your yard.

For seating, a stationary bench or two can be combined with movable furniture to give you maximum flexibility. A nearby fire pit (see pages 106–107) can be a focal point for evening entertaining. As a final touch, low-voltage lighting can give you just enough illumination. Hang lanterns or string lights to creative a festive atmosphere for parties or other gatherings.

BUILDING A GRILLWORK SCREEN

Here's a project that can add privacy to an outdoor living area, buffer a prevailing wind, or hide an unsightly view. In addition, it will be an ideal place to plant climbing flowers or vines. This project uses readily available lumber and is easy to build.

This simple design can be modified to suit your needs. Once the posts and 1×6s are in place, you can hold up 2×2 pieces in various configurations until you find an attractive pattern. Move the pieces closer together or farther apart, depending on how much privacy you want and what type of climbing plants you will be using. Or use ready-made lattice panels instead of 2×2s.

The overall size of the project is flexible as well: The overall width can be 6 to 10 feet; the height can be 5 to 8 feet.

Choose rot-resistant lumber, such as brown pressure-treated or the heartwood of cedar or redwood. If you plan to paint your trellis, you'll have an easier time of it and get better results if you paint the pieces before assembling them—it's hard to avoid drips when painting all those intersecting pieces. With a less drip-prone product like stain or sealer, you can apply your finish after the screen is constructed.

YOU'LL NEED

TIME: About a day.
SKILLS: Measuring and cutting, plumbing posts, digging postholes, attaching with galvanized screws or nails.
TOOLS: Circular saw, drill, hammer, posthole digger, level.

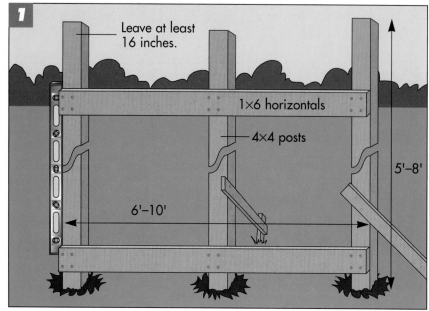

Leave at least 16 inches.

1×6 horizontals

4×4 posts

5'-8'

6'-10'

1. Set posts and horizontals.
Dig all three postholes at least 30 inches deep. Shovel in several inches of gravel, and set the two outside posts in the holes. Check the posts for plumb in both directions, and make sure they line up. Temporarily brace them using stakes driven into the ground. Fasten two 1×6s, one a couple of inches above the ground and the other near the top (leave at least 16 inches for the overhead structure). Drive four screws into each joint. Center the middle post and attach it to the 1×6s as well. If you will be setting the posts in soil only, tamp them in place now. If you will be using concrete, wait until the structure is built.

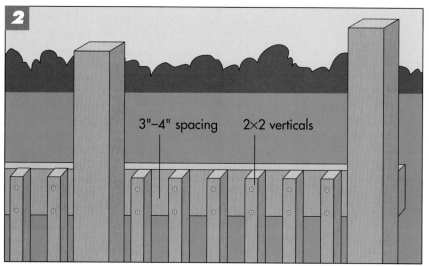

3"–4" spacing   2×2 verticals

2. Install verticals.
Plan the spacing so that there are about 3 to 4 inches between pieces. Be sure the spacing between the outermost 2×2 vertical and its adjacent post is also 3 to 4 inches. Install the verticals by drilling pilot holes and driving two 2-inch deck screws into each joint, through the 2×2 and into the 1×6. The structure will be a little wobbly now, but will become more steady as you add more support pieces.

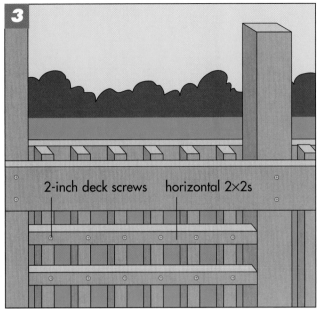

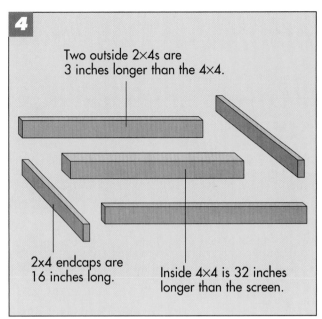

3. Add horizontals.

Lay out the horizontal 2×2s; usually it is best to use the same spacing as for the verticals so that the holes are square. Cut 2×2s to fit snugly between the posts, up against the inside faces of the posts. Install them by driving a 2-inch deck screw into each joint. Add the other 1×6 pieces with 2-inch screws.

4. Build the top section.

Measure up from the top 1×6s about 16 inches. Level across and cut off the tops of all three posts. Cut a 4×4 about 32 inches longer than the width of the screen; two 2×4s, 3 inches longer than the 4×4; and two 2×4s at 16 inches. Assemble them in a simple box. Attach all the joints with 3-inch deck screws, drilling pilot holes near the edges of boards.

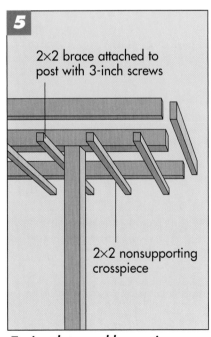

5. Attach top, add crosspieces.

Set the top section on top of the posts, overhanging the same distance on both ends. At each post, add a 2×2 brace, attaching with 3-inch screws. Attach additional 2×2s, evenly spaced.

6. Finish or paint, plant vines.

Give the whole structure a coat or two of paint, stain, or sealer. Do a thorough job; you won't want to have to remove vines to refinish the grillwork screen later.

Planting is the final step. For a screen with widely spaced lattice pieces, choose climbing plants that are bushy or that cling well, such as roses or clematis.

BUILDING BASIC TRELLISES

A trellis is any structure that contains lattice; lattice is any combination of materials that allows light to filter through and provides a place for plants to climb. Thousands of trellis designs are possible, using a wide variety of materials. Usually, the lattice of a trellis is made up of thin, evenly crisscrossed material, often wood strips. Large or patterned pieces can also make a trellis.

The design shown at right can be built in a few hours using commonly available materials. Use rot-resistant lumber, and soak the 2×4 ends that go into the soil with a sealer/preservative. Use 1⅝-inch deck screws to fasten the horizontal 1×2s to the 2×4 posts, then to the three verticals. Drill pilot holes if there is any danger of cracking the wood.

Set the 2×4 posts in holes 20 to 30 inches deep, and firmly tamp soil back in the hole, keeping them fairly plumb as you work. Or support the posts with fence stakes: Set the structure in place, pound the stakes into the ground, and tie the posts to the stakes with copper wire. With this arrangement, you can remove the structure at the end of the summer and store it until spring.

2×4 posts

1×2 lattice pieces

Use fence stakes if posts aren't set at least 20 inches in the ground.

YOU'LL NEED

TIME: For any of these three designs, just a few hours.
SKILLS: Basic carpentry.
TOOLS: Posthole digger, drill, saw, wire cutters.

A-frame with chicken wire.

Since the triangular design of this garden trellis makes it very stable, it doesn't need to be anchored to the ground unless you have exceptionally high winds in your area. Build each side on a flat surface, spacing the horizontal pieces evenly and attaching them to 6-foot vertical supports that are spaced 4 feet apart. Use two 3-inch deck screws at each joint. Lean the two sides against each other at the top; keep them about 5 feet apart at the bottom, and drape chicken wire over the whole structure. Flatten the chicken wire, holding it snug to the frame, and attach the wire with a staple every foot or so on all the 2×4s.

With the chicken wire acting as a hinge, you can fold this structure up and move it easily.

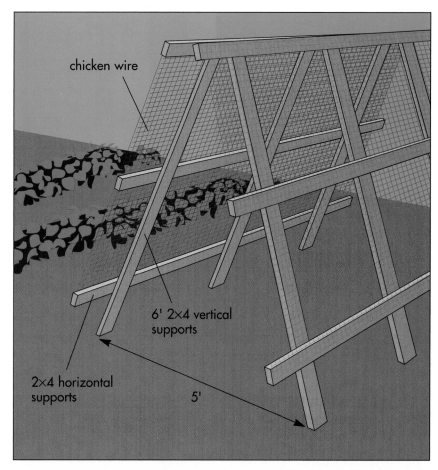

chicken wire

6' 2×4 vertical supports

2×4 horizontal supports

5'

Wire mesh planting bed.

This project is ideal for squash and other climbing vegetables. The timbers can be permanent parts of your garden while the wire mesh may need to be replaced every few years. For the border of the planting bed, use at least 1× pressure-treated lumber supported with 2×2 stakes.

Use landscaping timbers for a more permanent but less space-conserving border. The width of the timbers will eat up a surprising amount of square footage in a small garden. Keep them in place by boring holes every 3 feet and pounding in 2-foot-long pieces of rebar.

For the climbing lattice, purchase 4-inch wire mesh—the type that is used for reinforcing concrete. Fasten it to the insides of the planting bed with U-shape wire fasteners, taking care not to crimp the wire as you bend it over.

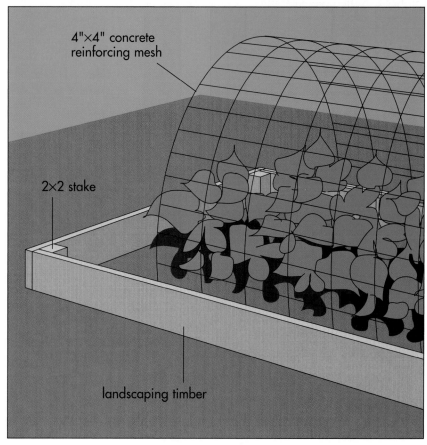

4"×4" concrete reinforcing mesh

2×2 stake

landscaping timber

MAKING BENTWOOD TRELLISES

Bentwood furniture has been an American tradition for hundreds of years. Using only branches of various thicknesses and working quickly, craftsmen fashioned chairs and tables that have lasted for years. Most of us will never learn how to make a rocking chair, but with a little patience we can make a rustic trellis or two. And it will cost next to nothing in materials.

The first step is to find the materials. You will need to scavenge. Check with tree trimmers or nurseries; look in swampy areas or along rivers; pick up fallen branches after a storm; or just look around your own property. When a tree has been cut down, often its stump will send up shoots that are easily worked. Choose branches that are still green so they will bend easily.

Cedar, cypress, and willow are all easy to work with and long-lasting. Oak, maple, hickory, and apple also work well. Other woods, such as elm, sycamore, mulberry, peach, and grapevines, are easy to work with but will only last for a year or two. Just about any wood that is easily bent will be good enough to practice on. After you get good at it, you can look for higher-quality materials.

The greener the wood, the better. Plan to start building your trellis within a day of cutting the wood from its live source. Soaking this kind of wood in water does not usually do much good.

To tie the pieces together, a skilled craftsman may be able to use thin branches, but beginners should use wire and nails. Copper wire will turn an attractive green with time.

Here are some classic bentwood trellis designs, all of them 6 to 8 feet tall. If you want a smaller version, scale back the number of pieces, so you don't end up trying to twist branches into impossibly tight curves.

Prepare an open area in which to work. A driveway or garage floor will do, but you will have a more pleasant time with a picnic table or large workbench.

1. Lay out a basic frame.
On a convenient working surface, lay out two long vertical pieces, about 2 feet apart for a 6- to 8-foot-high trellis. Lay the bottom and top horizontals on top, and stand back to see that everything looks square and symmetrical.

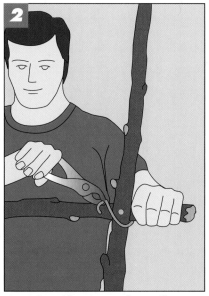

2. Join with wire and a nail.
Pound a single nail into each joint. If a nail pokes through, bend its tip over with a hammer. Eyeball the structure again for square, and wrap each joint with wire. Begin by wrapping by hand, looping the wire around in a crossing pattern. Twist tight with lineman's pliers.

3. Join the curved top pieces.
This may be a bit difficult until you get the knack. You may need a helper. Bend the top of one vertical piece, then the other, and hold them together in a smooth arch. Make adjustments until it looks right. Attach each piece with wire wrapped around both of its ends and twisted tight with pliers.

4. Fill in the design.

Once you have made a rectangle with a curved top, you can proceed to make any of a great number of designs. Start with the verticals. Many designs call for a center vertical, and others require two outside pieces. Then add horizontal or angle pieces. Attach all joints with a nail and wire where possible, and with wire only in all other joints.

5. Add braces where needed.

Diagonal pieces can be added for strength, but place them in a symmetrical pattern to integrate them into the design. Bentwood trellises are very informal, no one expects anything close to precision, but try to balance materials—use pieces of the same width on either side, for instance.

6. Anchor to the ground.

Metal fence stakes are the easiest to use and are unobtrusive, but wooden stakes will work, too. A 4½-foot metal stake, driven 2 feet into the ground, will probably be strong enough. Drive the stakes into the ground the same distance apart as your main vertical pieces. Wire the verticals to the stakes in at least two places

Try these designs.

A design with mostly straight pieces, such as the one on the right, will be easier to make than one that calls for lots of curves.

Curved ends that are not attached to another piece (see the heart inside the middle trellis) are difficult; you will have to tie them in place for a few

days until they harden into position. For the design at left, the six short curved pieces in the middle must be bent and allowed to harden before attaching.

CHOOSING BENCH AND PLANTER DESIGNS

A flower box is an excellent first project if you are new to do-i t-yourself carpentry. Because it is a simple structure with no critical joints or dimensions to fuss over, you'll be able to build it and possibly stock it with flowers on the same day. You can fill a flower box with soil and plant it directly with annuals, perennials, or herbs. Or use the box as a decorative holder for plastic or clay flowerpots. That way, you can keep it filled with blooming plants throughout the growing season. Another option is to build several small planters that can be rotated as flowers come in and out of bloom.

Benches are somewhat more complicated to build, but a basic bench is something most modestly ambitious do-it-yourselfers can build in a weekend.

ABOVE: *Flower boxes don't have to be fancy to be effective. These rough boxes made of old cedar planks fit right into an informal garden. See pages 62–67 for a variety of flower boxes and planters, ranging from the simple to the complicated, that you can build yourself.*

LEFT: *The curved-back bench with its matching arbor is not only an eye-catching feature for a backyard, but a shady place to relax. While purchasing a ready-made bench is both time- and cost-effective, making your own bench allows you to adapt the design to match or complement other structures in your yard. For bench projects you can make, see pages 50–59 and page 63.*

ABOVE: *This Adirondack-style bench and chair have high tilted backs that make them more comfortable than most all-wood seats. A variation on this theme is shown on pages 60–61.*

ABOVE RIGHT: *A garden bench is an ideal addition to a quiet retreat in your yard. See pages 56–57 for a similar yet simpler bench project.*

RIGHT: *Window-box planters are an ideal way to add color and detail to your home. To make an ornamental window box like the one at right, see page 67.*

BELOW: *The legs on this handsome planter help air to circulate under the planter and prevent rot.*

CONSTRUCTING A BASIC BENCH

Regardless of how simple the bench design is, rigidity must be built in to prevent the piece from wiggling. If the bench will be stationary, you might be able to attach it to a deck railing or sink posts into the ground. But for a stand-alone bench, either use a series of massive supports (as in the design on page 51), or supply angled braces, as in this design.

YOU'LL NEED

TIME: Most of a day.
SKILLS: Measuring and squaring, accurate cutting, attaching with screws or bolts.
TOOLS: Circular saw, drill, tape measure, square.

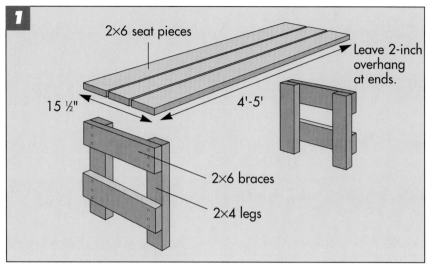

1

2×6 seat pieces

Leave 2-inch overhang at ends.

15 ½"

4'-5'

2×6 braces

2×4 legs

1. Make supports and add seat.
Cut four legs to the height of your bench, minus 1½ inches (a height of 17 inches is standard). Cut four 2×6 braces, 16 inches long. Construct the two supports by attaching the braces to the legs as shown. Drill pilot holes and drive three 2½-inch deck screws into each joint.

Cut three 2×6 seat pieces, no more than 5 feet long, and set them on top of the supports, allowing a 2-inch overhang on each end. Drive two 3-inch deck screws into each joint. The structure will be a bit unsteady at this point.

2. Make the long braces.
Check to see that the legs are square to the seat pieces. Hold a piece of 2×4 against a leg and the seat, as shown, so that it extends 6 inches or so past the middle of the bench. Mark the two ends for angle cuts. Cut, check to see if it will fit, and use it as a template for a second brace.

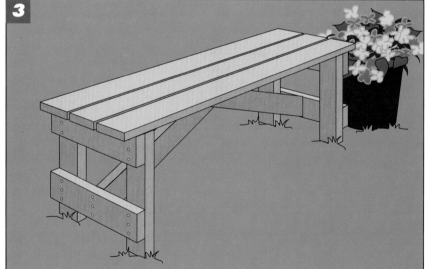

3. Add the long braces.
Position the long braces so that they run past each other in the center of the bench. Attach them to the cross-braces with 3-inch deck screws, and to the middle seat piece by drilling pilot holes and driving screws upward

through the brace and into the seat piece, taking care that they do not poke up through the seat. Sand all the edges of the bench smooth, taking special care with the ends of the seat pieces. Brush on sealer/preservative, or give it at least two coats of paint.

BUILDING A SLATTED BENCH

This one has solid-looking supports. It can be attached to a deck or used as a movable piece of furniture. The seat, made of eight 2×2s, is more complicated to build than one made with a few 2×6s, but it has a pleasingly hand-crafted look.

Take care when choosing the 4×4s. They need to be nearly free of cracks because you will be using very short pieces. A high grade of redwood will cost more but will probably perform much better than standard pressure-treated lumber.

YOU'LL NEED

TIME: Most of a day.
SKILLS: Measuring and squaring, cutting, boring long holes.
TOOLS: Circular saw, drill with long bit, socket wrench, square.

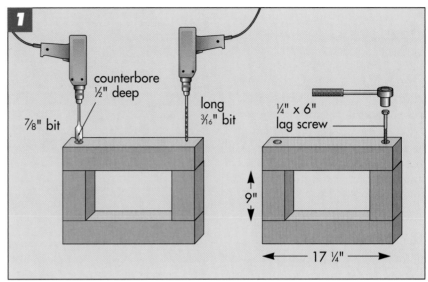

1. Make the supports.
For each support, cut two 4×4s to 9 inches and two to 17¼ inches. Assemble the pieces building-block style. At each joint, drill a pilot hole for a lag screw. Take care that the pieces remain flush with each other as you work. To ensure that the screw heads do not protrude above the surface of the wood, drill a second counterbore hole, about ½ inch deep, using a ⅞-inch bit.

Place washers on the screws and ratchet them tight. Set the supports on a flat surface with the screw heads on top and bottom, so they will not show.

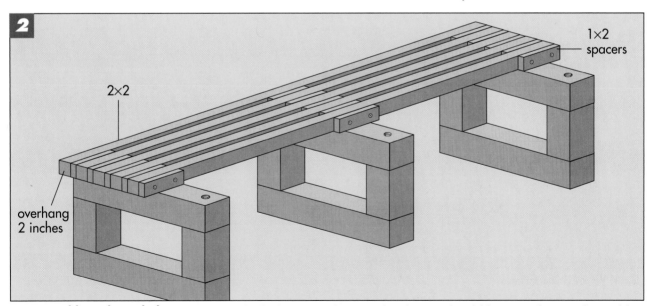

2. Assemble and attach the seat.
Cut 8 2×2s to the length of the bench plus 4 inches, and 21 pieces of 1×2 to 6 inches. Attach a 2×2, so its face is flush with the faces of the supports and it overhangs the ends by 2 inches, by drilling a pilot hole and angle-driving a 2-inch deck screw. Then sandwich pieces as shown, alternating 2×2s with 1×2 spacers. On every other piece, drive an angled screw into the support or a 3-inch screw horizontally, to tie several seat pieces together. By the time you've attached the eighth 2×2, the seat should be very close to the width of the supports. If the seat is a little narrower, add a piece of cedar shim to the last spacer, so it comes out right. Sand the seat thoroughly, and apply a coat or two of sealer/preservative.

BUILDING A WRAPAROUND TREE BENCH

A feature like this can turn a secluded spot in your backyard into a relaxing place to sit and read, putting a shady area to good use.

Construction will take some patience and unusual methods, but it is not difficult if you follow the steps. For the best results, build the bench in two sections, and then determine where to place the postholes by holding the bench temporarily in place.

YOU'LL NEED

TIME: One or two days.
SKILLS: Measuring and marking for odd angles, precise cutting, digging postholes, fastening with screws and bolts.
TOOLS: Circular saw and power miter saw or radial-arm saw (you can rent one), speed square, posthole digger, drill.

The length of this side equals the diameter of your tree.

18"

30°

1. Measure tree and cut 6 pieces.
Choose a tree that is not leaning heavily and has no visible roots.

Measure the tree's diameter 18 inches from the ground. Wrap a string around the tree and measure the string; this is the circumference. Divide by 3 (or pi, 3.14) to get the diameter.

Cut six pieces of 2×4 to be used as the seat pieces closest to the tree. For each, make the longest side as long as the diameter of your tree; this creates a tree bench that leaves room for the tree to grow. (If you have a fast-growing tree, add an inch or two.) Cut each end to exactly 30 degrees. Use a power miter saw or radial-arm saw to make the cuts; test with scrap pieces to make sure the angle is precise.

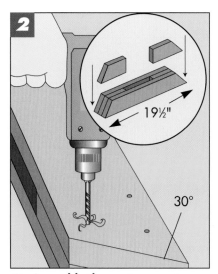

19½"

30°

2. Assemble the seat supports.
Construct six supports out of 2×4s: Sandwich two 6-inch-long pieces between two 19½-inch-long pieces. Some faces of these will show, so make sure the ends are evenly cut and all three pieces are flush. Drill pilot holes and drive 3-inch screws from either side.

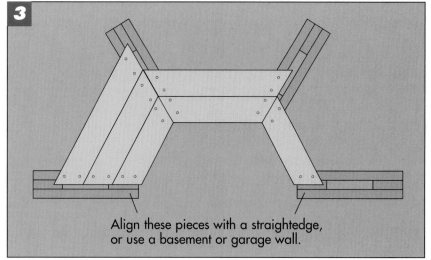

Align these pieces with a straightedge, or use a basement or garage wall.

3. Build the first half-section.
On a large flat surface, lay out the first seat section, using four seat supports and three of the inside seat pieces. Adjust so they fit together tightly, and the two outer supports line up in a straight line.

Cut the rest of the boards to fit, all with 30-degree cuts on each end. You may need to hold them and measure in place. Work carefully, testing as you go. After positioning the pieces tightly, attach them to the supports by drilling pilot holes and using 3-inch deck screws.

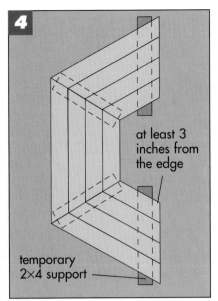

at least 3 inches from the edge

temporary 2×4 support

4. Build the second half-section.

The second section will have only two seat supports, so screw a piece of 2×4 onto the bottom of each end to temporarily hold it together while you assemble the bench; you will take these pieces out after the bench is built.

plumb bob

5. Locate and dig the postholes.

Set the two sections in place by resting them on chairs. To determine the location of each posthole, hang a plumb bob (you can use a chalk line) from the center of each seat support, and dig up a little turf or mark the spot directly below the plumb

bob. You may need to shift the whole assembly to avoid roots.

Dig the postholes about 24 inches deep. Do not cut any tree roots that are larger than 1 inch in diameter. If necessary, leave some postholes shallow. Shovel 2 inches of gravel into the bottom of each hole to promote drainage.

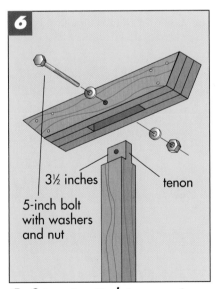

3½ inches   tenon

5-inch bolt with washers and nut

6. Cut posts, attach to supports.

Cut six 4×4 pressure-treated posts to the depth of each hole, plus 16 inches. Cut a tenon on one end, as shown, so the post will fit tightly into the seat support. (To do this, set your circular saw blade 1 inch deep, cut a series of lines on each end, and clean out with a chisel.) Install each post with a bolt.

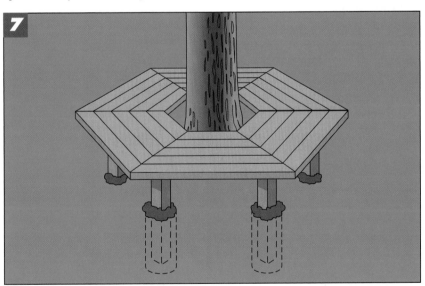

7. Install the bench.

With a helper, set the section with the four seat supports in place, inserting the posts into the holes. Then lower the other section into place. You will need to spend some time making adjustments—adding or removing dirt here and there—until the bench is reasonably level in all directions. Drill pilot holes and drive screws

to connect the second section to the first. Remove the temporary 2×4 braces. Shovel 8 inches of soil into each hole. Tamp firmly with a pole or 2×4, then repeat until the dirt is mounded up so water will run away from the post.

Sand all edges smooth so there will be no splinters. Brush on a coat or two of sealer/preservative, or apply paint.

MAKING AN ARBOR BENCH

With the addition of some climbing plants, this arbor bench makes a delightful retreat. Cutting the rafters so the resulting arch is smooth is the most difficult part of this project.

Once the curved pieces are cut, building this structure is no more difficult than making a straightforward arbor. Use high-quality, rot-resistant lumber, such as the heartwood of redwood or cedar. Avoid any rough pieces or pieces with large knots.

YOU'LL NEED

TIME: About a day and a half.
SKILLS: Measuring and squaring, cutting smooth curves, digging postholes, fastening with screws.
TOOLS: High-quality sabersaw, circular saw or power miter box, level, posthole digger, drill.

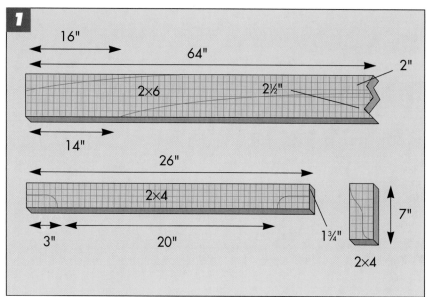

1. Cut the curved pieces.
To make the templates for these pieces, use large pieces of cardboard or paper; you may have to tape some pieces together. For the rafters, you will need a template 32 inches long, so you can use it on both halves. For the top pieces, you need only a template for one end cut. Mark a grid, draw freehand, and cut out carefully with a utility knife. Cut the 2×6s and 2×4s to length. For the curved cuts, use a professional-quality sabersaw. Once you have one of each type that looks good, use it as a template for the others. Sand the pieces smooth.

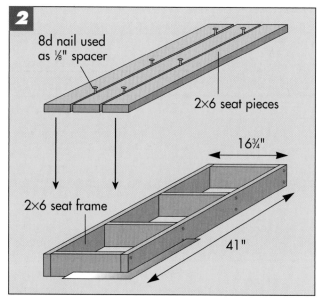

2. Build the seat.
Construct a 2×6 frame 41 inches by 16¾ inches. Check it for square. Drive two 3-inch screws at each joint. Cut three 2×6 boards to 41 inches for the seat. Using 8d nails as spacers between the seat pieces, attach the pieces so their ends are flush with the frame and their sides overhang the frame evenly.

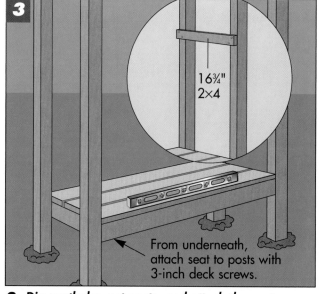

3. Dig postholes, set posts, and attach the seat.
Set the bench on the ground and mark for four postholes. Dig the holes at least 30 inches deep. Plumb the posts and brace them until you level and attach the seat piece to the four posts with 3-inch deck screws. Fasten the top 2×4 braces about 76 inches above the ground using 3-inch deck screws.

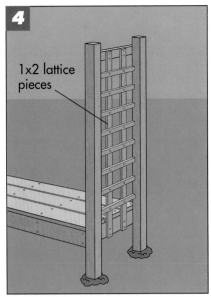

4. Build the lattice.
Cut the posts to a level height (see page 34). On each side, evenly space two 1×2 vertical pieces that run flush to the top of the 2×4 brace and the bottom of the bench frame. Fill in with horizontal 1×2s, cut to fit between the posts. Space them consistently. Attach them to the vertical 1×2s (not to the posts) with a 1⅝-inch screw at each joint.

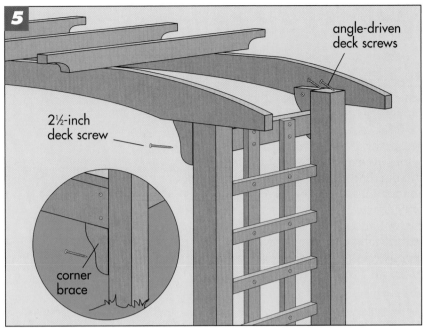

5. Add rafters and corner braces.
Set the front rafter in place, the bottom edge about 2 inches below the top of the posts. Attach it to the posts from behind by drilling pilot holes and angle-driving 2½-inch deck screws. Take care that the screws do not poke through the front of the rafter. Work carefully to avoid splitting the rafters. Add the decorative corner braces beneath the seat frame and the rafters. For each, drill pilot holes, hold the braces in place, and drive 3-inch deck screws into the posts and bench frame pieces.

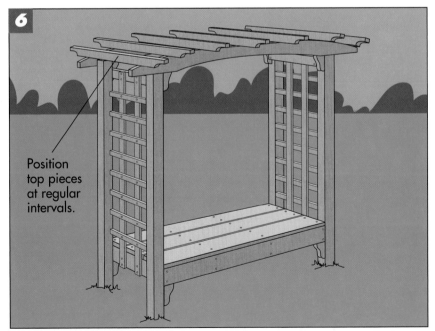

6. Finish with the top pieces.
Lay out the top pieces on the rafters so they are at regular intervals. Attach them to the rafters with angle-driven screws. Sand the seat and the inside face of the posts smooth. Finish the arbored bench with a couple of coats of paint or sealer/preservative. Plant climbing vines at either end to grow up the lattice.

EXPERTS' INSIGHT

MAINTAINING A TRELLIS
Moisture trapped on the lattice pieces can rot your trellis. Give it two coats of long-lasting finish before planting the vine that will grow up the trellis. Inspect it once a year a day or two after a rainfall. If water has soaked into the wood rather than beading on the surface, it's time to recoat. Delicately remove the vines from the trellis in order to get them out of the way for refinishing. Your plant will probably survive if you work carefully. Inspect your posts as well. If a puddle forms around the post, mound well-tamped soil so that water will run away.

MAKING A SCALLOP-BACK BENCH

This attractive bench project gives you the chance to do some basic furniture making without having to execute complex joints. Use clear or nearly clear redwood or cedar. You may have to ask your lumberyard to mill a ¾×8 (1×7½ inch actual dimension) for the back and 3×3s (2½×2½ inch actual dimension) for the legs. If this is too difficult, you can substitute a 2×8 for the back and 4×4s for the legs. Decking boards of ¾×6 are readily available in cedar, but you may have to special-order for redwood.

YOU'LL NEED

TIME: About a day and a half.
SKILLS: Accurate measuring and squaring, cutting smooth curves.
TOOLS: Power miter saw or radial-arm saw, circular saw, drill, good-quality sabersaw.

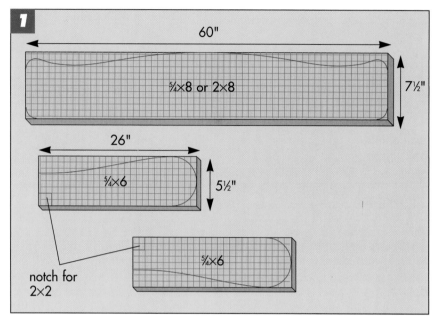

1. Cut the back and armrests.
Make cardboard templates of the patterns shown above, and transfer them to the lumber. If ¾×8 is difficult to find, use 2×8. Trace the patterns and cut carefully with a sabersaw. Use coarse (50–60 grit) sandpaper to round the edges (except the post notch) of these pieces, then finish them with medium (80–100) and then fine (120–150) sandpaper.

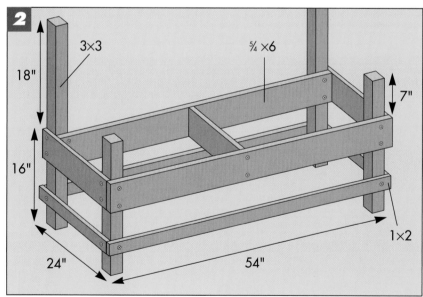

2. Construct the frame.
Using ¾×6, 3×3, and 1×2, build a frame as shown. You may want to make the notches for the rear posts (step 4) before you build the frame. Note that the front (shorter) posts are inside the frame, while the rear (taller) posts sit behind the main frame. Check for square as you work. Attach all the pieces with 2-inch decking screws; drill pilot holes wherever you will drive a screw near the end of a board. Cut three ¾×6 pieces to 56 inches for the seat.

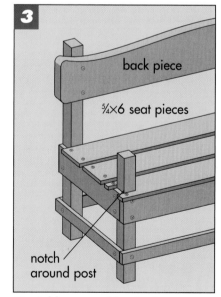

3. Add seat and back pieces.
Arrange the seat pieces so they overhang the frame by an inch on the sides and front. Notch around the front posts. Attach the pieces to the frame with 2½-inch screws. Install the back piece so that it overhangs the same distance on both posts.

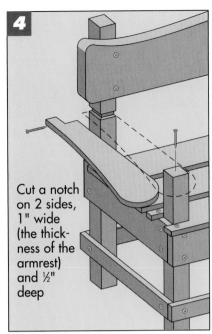

4

Cut a notch on 2 sides, 1" wide (the thickness of the armrest) and ½" deep

5

4. Add armrests.

Make a ½-inch-deep notch on two sides of each rear post. Carefully cut several passes with a circular saw and clean out with a chisel. Slip the armrest into the notch, and rest it on top of the front post. Fasten with 2-inch deck screws, drilling pilot holes to prevent splits.

5. Sand and finish.

Complete sanding all of the edges so the bench will be free of potential splinters. To retain the natural look of the wood, brush on a sealer/preservative with a light stain. For a more formal garden setting, give the the bench a couple coats of exterior enamel. This bench is ideal for a secluded area just off a flagstone path or graveled walkway.

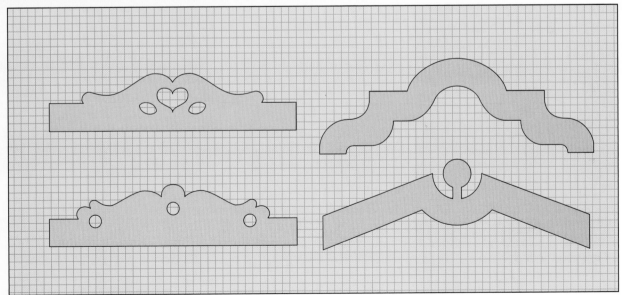

Alternative back designs

The back piece gives the bench its distinctive look, so you may want to come up with your own design. It should be symmetrical—the right half mirrors the left half. Don't be afraid to use your imagination, but avoid overly ornate designs; a few simple curves usually make the best statement. To ensure that the back piece will be strong enough, make sure that at least half of the board's width carries all the way through.

BUILDING A BENCH SWING

A bench like this will be one of your family's favorite spots in your yard or on your porch. The steps for building this project aren't difficult, but they must be done with precision. A bench that hangs suspended from four points and gets pushed needs to be built well. Make sure every screw is attached firmly and without splitting the wood. Cut the pieces accurately, so they fit together tightly, and use a strong wood, such as clear fir.

YOU'LL NEED

TIME: About a day and a half.
SKILLS: Precise measuring, squaring, cutting (especially lap joints), fastening with screws.
TOOLS: Power miter or radial-arm saw, drill, square, socket wrench.

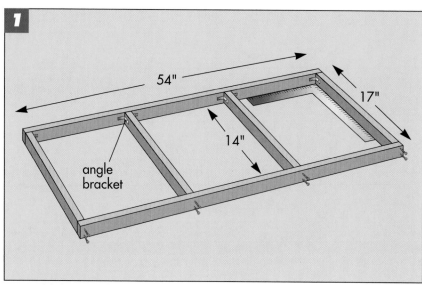

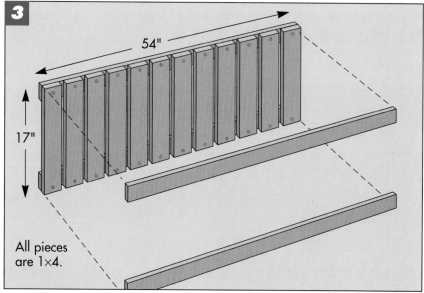

1. Build the seat frame.
Cut two 2×3s to 54 inches, and four to 14 inches. Carefully assemble the pieces to form a strong frame. Use a square as you work, and make sure the whole structure lies flat. Drill pilot holes before driving two 3-inch deck screws into each joint. On the insides of the joints, reinforce with angle brackets.

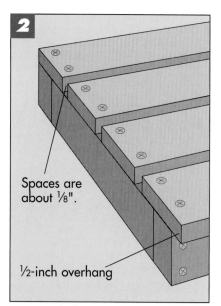

Spaces are about ⅛".

½-inch overhang

2. Attach the seat pieces.
Cut four 1×4s to 54 inches, space them evenly on the frame so that the ends are flush and the front piece overhangs ½ inch. Drill pilot holes and attach using two 2-inch deck screws at each joint. Set each screw so the head is slightly sunk below the surface of the wood. (You don't want water to puddle over the screw heads.)

All pieces are 1×4.

3. Build the back.
Make the back by sandwiching vertical 1×4s between horizontal 1×4s. Cut four 1×4s to 54 inches, and 12 1×4s to 17 inches. Lay two of the long pieces on a flat, well-swept surface, parallel to each other and square. Lay the 12 short pieces on the long pieces, flush at the top and bottom with the edges of the long pieces. Make the two outside pieces flush with the ends of the long pieces and see that all the pieces are consistently spaced, with about ½-inch gaps. Attach with one 1¼-inch deck screw per joint. Recheck for square. Add the top pieces, flush at the edges. Drill pilot holes and attach the pieces using two 2-inch deck screws per joint.

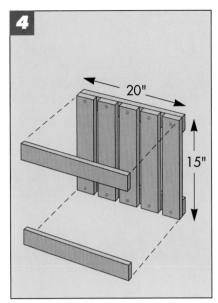

4. Build the arms.

For each arm, cut four 1×4s to 20 inches and five more to 15 inches. Sandwich the pieces together as you did for the back (step 3). Here, the gaps between the verticals will be about ⅝ inch.

Give the back and the arms a thorough sanding. Round off all the corners so there will be no sharp edges.

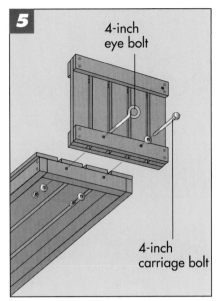

5. Attach the arms.

Lay the seat on a flat surface, and position one arm against it, so its front edge runs an inch past the front of the seat frame. Fasten the arm to the seat frame with a 4-inch carriage bolt in the rear and a 4-inch eye bolt in front. Flip the seat up and drive several 3-inch deck screws. Repeat on the other side.

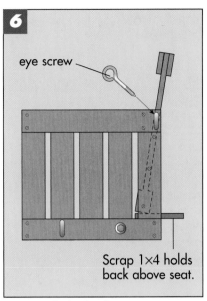

6. Attach the back.

With a helper or two, slip the back in place. Use scrap pieces of 1×4 to hold the back ¾ inch above the seat surface. Tilt the back for comfort, as shown. Attach the back to the arms by drilling pilot holes and driving 3-inch deck screws. At the point where the top of the arm meets the back, drive a 4-inch eye screw.

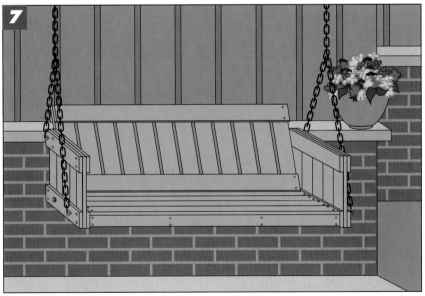

7. Attach the hooks and hang.

Sand the bench free of splinters, and apply finish or paint. Attach chain to the eye hooks and bolts, and suspend from two eye hooks driven into very solid material overhead. Position the overhead hooks so that the chain angles slightly away from the swing on either side. You will need to adjust the chain until you get just the right angle. Squeeze the hooks tight with pliers to ensure that the chain cannot pop out.

EXPERTS' INSIGHT

WHERE TO HANG A SWINGING BENCH

If kids will play on the swing, provide plenty of room for swinging back and forth. How far they can swing will depend on the length of the chain. Don't position the swing near a window or breakable objects.

When locating a swing on a porch that has a ceiling, you will need to find the joists; Do not attach the bench to just the 1x beaded board or other ceiling materials. Use a stud finder or tap with a hammer to find joists. Drive the hooks into the center of the joists.

MAKING AN ADIRONDACK CHAIR

Here's a classic design that's relatively easy to build. With its contoured seat, it's a chair designed for hours of comfortable sitting and relaxing.

Use wood that is resistant to rot and free of large knots and blemishes. The dark heartwood of redwood or cedar is an excellent choice; it will look great stained and sealed. Or use select grade pressure-treated wood that has been kiln-dried after treatment (KDAT), and paint it.

YOU'LL NEED

TIME: A day to cut the pieces and assemble the chair.
SKILLS: Accurate measuring and cutting, drilling pilot holes, and driving screws.
TOOLS: Circular or tablesaw, sabersaw, drill, square, compass, C-clamps.

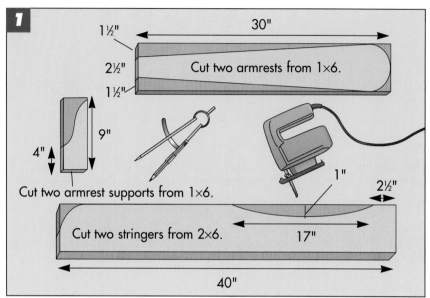

1. Cut the curved pieces.
Wherever you need two pieces that are the same, use the first piece as a template for the other. Use a compass to mark for the rounded end of the first arm piece. Draw the curved line of the stringer freehand, pressing lightly with the pencil and erasing and starting again until you get a smooth curve. The armrest supports do not have to be this exact shape; draw a design that pleases you.

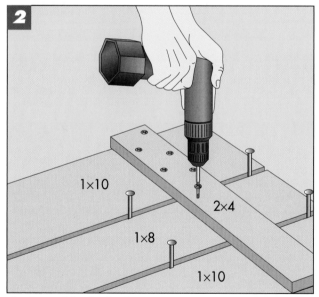

2. Assemble the back.
Cut two pieces of 1×10 and one 1×8 to 30 inches. Lay them next to each other on a flat surface with the 1×8 in the middle. Use spacers to maintain ¼-inch gaps between the boards, and make sure they are square to each other. Lay two 2×4 braces on top. They can overhang; you will cut them later. Attach the braces with polyurethane glue and 2-inch screws. Take care that the screws do not poke through.

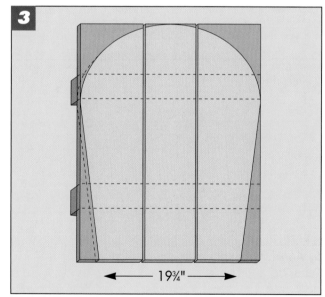

3. Cut the back.
Turn the back assembly right-side up. Mark for the arching upper cut using a notched wood compass (page 13). Draw the two lower cut lines with a straightedge, taking care that the bottom width is 19¾ inches. Cut the straight lines with a circular saw, and use a sabersaw for the curved cut. Before cutting, make sure you will not be cutting through any screws; remove some if necessary.

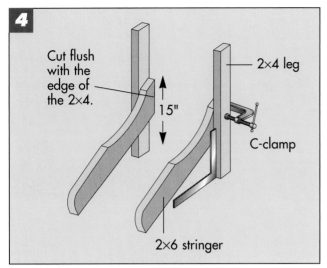

Cut flush with the edge of the 2×4.

15"

2×4 leg

C-clamp

2×6 stringer

4. Assemble the legs and stringers.

Cut two 2×4s to 24 inches. Make a mark 15 inches from the bottom of one 2×4, and hold it next to a framing square on a level surface. Position one of the stringers that you cut in step one so that its upper corner is at the 15-inch mark, and clamp it. Drill pilot holes and drive several 2½-inch decking screws. Cut the leading edge of the stringer flush with the edge of the 2×4. Repeat for the other leg; remember to make one left leg and one right leg.

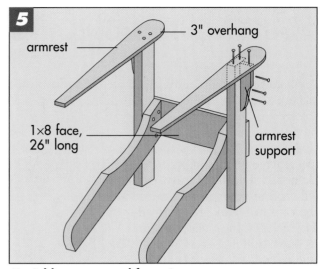

armrest

3" overhang

1×8 face, 26" long

armrest support

5. Add armrests and face piece.

Attach an armrest support to the side of each leg. Clamp in place so that the top edge is flush with the top of the leg. Carefully drive pilot and counterbore holes, and drive screws. Cut a piece of 1×8 to 26 inches, and attach it with screws to the front of the leg-and-stringer assemblies, so that the top edge is flush with the top of the stringer. Attach the arms to the top of the posts, so their front edges overhang the posts by 3 inches.

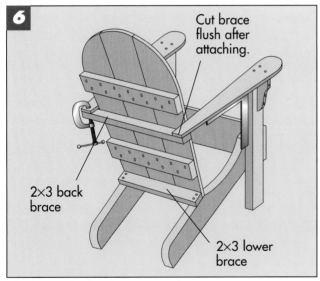

Cut brace flush after attaching.

2×3 back brace

2×3 lower brace

6. Attach the back.

Cut a 2×3 lower brace to 23 inches, and attach it to the stringers just at the end of the curved cuts. Have a helper hold the back in position while you drive screws to attach its bottom edge to the brace. Use a framing square to true up the armrests, and mark for the position of the 2×3 back brace. Cut it longer than needed, and attach it with screws driven through the 1× lumber. Attach the armrests to the back brace with two screws at each joint. It may help to use clamps while working. Cut the back brace flush on either side.

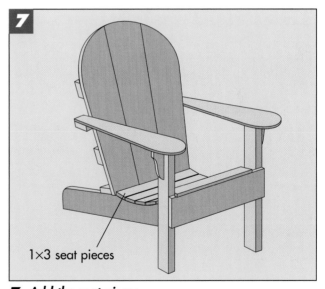

1×3 seat pieces

7. Add the seat pieces.

If you would like to change the angle of the back, move the bottom brace; back out the screws first. Cut six 1×3s to 23 inches, and position them on the seat so they are evenly spaced. Drill pilot holes and drive two 2-inch screws at each joint.

Fill any countersunk holes with wood filler or dowels. Sand so there is no possibility of splinters; round off any sharp corners. Apply paint or finish.

BUILDING A RAISED PLANTER

Choose or design a planter that harmonizes with your deck, patio, or house. If you want it to blend in so that only the flowers will be noticed, use the same materials and finish as your house or deck surfaces. Create visual interest by adding simple bands of 1×2 or other molding. On outdoor structures like planters, simple butt-jointed moldings usually look better than mitered joints, especially after a few years of wear and tear.

Develop a planting strategy. If you live in an area with mild winters, you may be able to plant perennials in a box—check with local nurseries. If you want to be able to move things around, build light planters, or use planters as holders for flower pots. Protect your deck or patio surface from the water that seeps out the bottom of a planter—it can cause ugly stains. Provide a pathway for the water to seep through the patio or deck, or place a water-holding trivet under the planter.

YOU'LL NEED

TIME: About two thirds of a day.
SKILLS: Basic carpentry.
TOOLS: Circular saw, drill, tape measure.

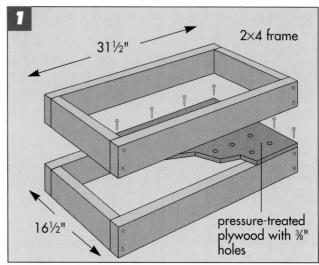

1. Build the frames, add plywood.
Use pressure-treated lumber and plywood that has a cca rating of .40 or more or the label says *ground contact*. Construct two simple frames out of 2×4s, both the same size. Check for square, and drive two 3-inch deck screws into each joint.

Cut a piece of pressure-treated plywood to fit, and fasten it to the bottom frame with 1⅝-inch deck screws. Drill a series of ⅜-inch holes in the plywood, so that water will be able to seep through easily.

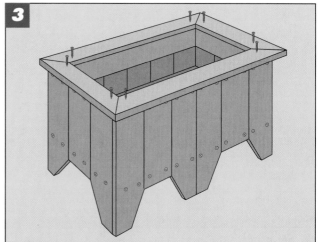

2. Cut and add side pieces.
Cut 12 legs with 45-degree cuts on one corner. The top of the miter cut will meet the bottom of the six straight-cut shorter pieces. Cut one piece, and use it as a template for the others. Cut shorter pieces to fill in. The dimensions shown will give you a planter that is 24 inches high. Attach to the frames with 1⅝-inch deck screws.

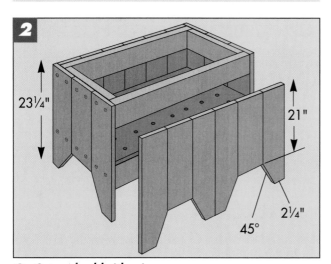

3. Add the top pieces.
Use 1×4s that are straight, dry, and have few knots. Hold in place, with the boards overhanging the front by an inch, and mark for mitered cuts, as shown, or cut the ends square and simply butt them together.

These top pieces come under a good deal of stress, so fasten them securely. Drill pilot holes and drive 2-inch deck screws, most of them into the frame and some into the side pieces.

Shovel in 4 to 6 inches of gravel, then fill with light soil that has plenty of organic matter.

MAKING A BENCH PLANTER

Benches and planters often sit side by side on a deck or patio, so why not build them together? This design uses stacked 2×4s for a solid, building-block sort of look. Here is a simple arrangement with two planters and one bench. You can easily modify this design to turn a corner and have three planters with two benches; the center planter will have both benches tied into it at 90-degree angles. Use rot-resistant lumber, and choose smooth sides for the top of the bench.

YOU'LL NEED

TIME: About a day.
SKILLS: Modest carpentry skills.
TOOLS: Circular saw, drill, square.

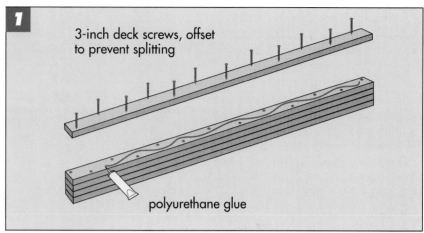

3-inch deck screws, offset to prevent splitting

polyurethane glue

1. Make the bench.
Laminate eight or more 2×4s, each no more than 8 feet long. Cut them all to the same length (the ends do not have to match exactly since they will not show). Stack them, apply a squiggle of polyurethane glue, and drive 3-inch deck screws every 6 inches in an alternating pattern to avoid splitting the wood. Use 2½-inch screws for the first piece, then use 3-inch screws. Glue and clamp the last piece rather than driving screws, so there will be no visible screw heads.

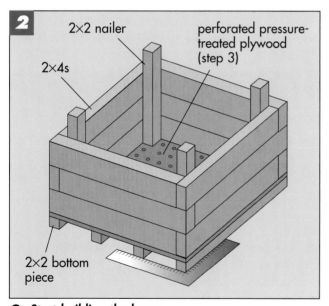

2×2 nailer
2×4s
perforated pressure-treated plywood (step 3)
2×2 bottom piece

2. Start building the boxes.
For a box 24 inches square and 21 inches tall, cut nineteen 2×4s to 22½ inches, four 2×2s to 24 inches, and four 2×2 nailers to 19½ inches.

Set the bottom 2×2s on a flat surface, evenly spaced to form a 24-inch square. With a helper or two, stack the first two courses of 2×4s in the pattern shown. Hold the pieces flush at their ends and tie them together by driving screws from the inside, through the nailers and into the 2×4s. To make the work easier, you can drive screws from the outside. Stack and attach three courses of 2×4s.

filler piece

3. Fasten them together.
After you have built the boxes three courses tall, set them in place and set the bench on top. Continue stacking and attaching the 2×4 planter pieces. Install filler pieces next to the bench.

Build the box five courses tall. Cut a piece of pressure-treated plywood to fit inside each planter, drill a series of ⅜-inch holes in it, and screw it to the bottom pieces. If you like, protect the sides of your 2×4s by stapling thick plastic sheeting to the inside of the planters. Fill with 4 to 6 inches of gravel, a sheet of weed blocking fabric, and then light soil rich in organic material.

CONSTRUCTING A SEMICIRCULAR PLANTER

With its unusual shape, this planter will be a focal point in your backyard or patio. It's not difficult to build, though you will spend some time marking and cutting the curved pieces.

There are no 2× framing pieces in this design; the 1×4s and plywood cutouts carry all the stress. It will be strong enough for a structure that is 3 feet by 3 feet, but no larger. Choose highly rot-resistant wood, and apply plenty of sealer-preservative to the inside bottom of the 1×4 pieces, because they will get wet.

YOU'LL NEED

TIME: Most of a day.
SKILLS: Measuring and squaring, marking and cutting smooth curves, fastening with screws.
TOOLS: Circular saw, sabersaw, square, drill.

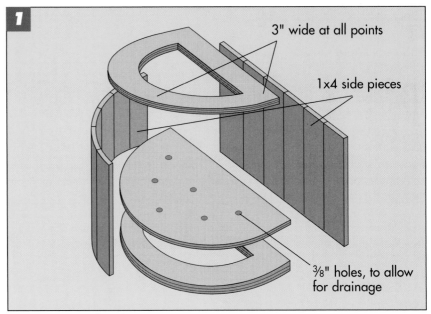

3" wide at all points

1x4 side pieces

⅜" holes, to allow for drainage

1. Cut plywood, side pieces.
Use a notched-wood or string-and-pencil compass (page 13) to mark the planter's contours on a sheet of ¾-inch pressure-treated plywood. Cut the plywood bottom pieces and drill a series of ⅜-inch drainage holes. Use it as a template for the top and bottom D-shaped pieces. Cut the top piece carefully using a piece of plywood free of large knots or other weak spots. Cut all the 1×4 side pieces to the same length; 18 inches is the recommended height.

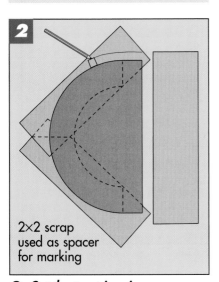

2×2 scrap used as spacer for marking

2. Cut the top trim pieces.
Depending on the size of your planter, use 2×10 or 2×12 to make the curve with two pieces. Use the top plywood piece and a scrap piece of 2×2 to mark for trim pieces that will overhang the sides by at least ½ inch. Cut with a sabersaw and sand smooth. Cut the straight trim piece as well.

3. Assemble the box.
Attach the top plywood piece to the underside of the trim pieces, using 2-inch deck screws. Set the bottom piece on 2× scraps, to hold it off the ground while you work. With a helper, attach side pieces to it with 2-inch deck screws.

Once you have most of them attached, carefully slip the top piece over the structure, so the trim overhangs the side pieces. Fasten the tops of the side pieces to the plywood and the top trim by drilling pilot holes and driving 3-inch screws at an upward angle.

Sand and finish. Place 6 inches of gravel in the bottom of the planter, then fill with light soil that is rich in organic material.

BUILDING A PLANTER WITH A SITTING LEDGE

Gardening is easy if you can sit right next to your flower bed. And sometimes it's pleasant to just sit near the foliage. This solid structure can easily provide a place for plants and the gardener alike.

This easy-to-build planter box can accommodate anything from flowers to a small vegetable patch. Bottom pieces facilitate air circulation to protect the base of the planter and—if the box is on a deck—the deck planking itself.

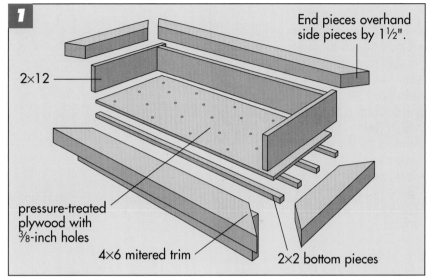

YOU'LL NEED

TIME: Several hours.
SKILLS: Measuring and squaring, cutting with a circular saw, attaching with screws.
TOOLS: Circular saw, drill, square.

1. Cut the pieces.
Choose rot resistant lumber for all pieces. Cut 2×2 bottom pieces and a sheet of pressure-treated plywood to form the base. The 2×12 end and side pieces will wrap around the plywood and sit on the 2×2s. Cut the end pieces 6 inches longer than the width of the plywood, so they run past the side pieces 1½ inches on each side. The box is capped with mitered 4×6 top trim. Use a speed square to mark for the 45-degree cuts; you will need to cut both sides with a circular saw.

2. Assemble and finish.
Drill a grid of ⅜-inch holes in the plywood. Place it on evenly spaced 2×2s, and attach with 1⅝-inch deck screws. Assemble the sides and ends, attaching to each other and to the 2×2 bottom pieces with 3-inch deck screws. Attach the mitered trim pieces together by drilling pilot holes and horizontally driving 3-inch deck screws. Drill pilot holes and drive 3-inch deck screws at an upward angle, from inside the box, through the 2×12s and into the 4×6s.

Sand all corners and edges smooth. Apply paint or sealer. Fill with several inches of gravel, followed by light soil that is rich in organic material.

EXPERTS' INSIGHT

GALVANIZED AND PLASTIC LINERS

Pressure-treated lumber and the heartwood of redwood or cedar will last a long time, especially if you allow for proper drainage and coat the wood with a sealer/preservative. But there are no guarantees that the wood will not become discolored or rot.

A custom-made galvanized liner placed in the finished planter will protect it. Build the planter, then have a sheet-metal company custom-make a liner with a drainage spout. Add holes for water to run out the bottom.

Or, buy a piece of pond liner fabric to fit your planter. This material is available at gardening shops and home centers.

MAKING WINDOW BOXES

This is a quick way to add charm to your home's exterior. Choose a spot that gets enough sun, but watch out for places that bake in the summer sun—a shallow box will need to be watered every day during the hot months. Use rot-resistant wood, and seal it well so it can stand the heat.

Determine the best height for your box. If the flowers will be tall, or if the view out of the window is important, you may want to lower it a foot or more below the windowsill.

YOU'LL NEED

TIME: Most of a day to build and hang a window box.
SKILLS: Basic carpentry.
TOOLS: Circular saw or power miter saw, sabersaw, drill, square, sanding block, hammer.

EXPERTS' INSIGHT

WAYS OF ATTACHING WINDOW BOXES

■ Though small, a window box can get quite heavy when it rains, so anchor it well. It will probably tend to pull away at the top of the box, so anchor the top directly, and support it with well-anchored brackets from beneath.

■ On a frame house, drive long screws through the top portion of the box into framing members of the house, which are usually easy to find under a window. Attach brackets in the same way.

■ On a masonry house, things get a bit tougher. Use masonry screws or lag shields, as described on page 16.

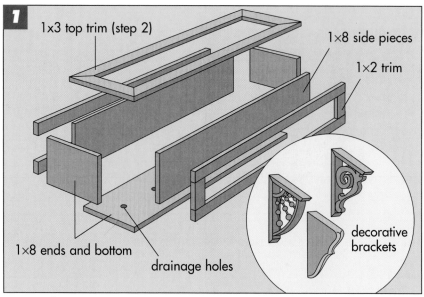

1x3 top trim (step 2)   1x8 side pieces   1x2 trim   1x8 ends and bottom   drainage holes   decorative brackets

1. Cut the pieces.

Cut the 1x8 bottom and sides to the length you want for your box—you may want to match the width of your window, including trim. Drill ⅜-inch drainage holes in the center, every 6 inches or so.

Cut the end pieces 1½ inches longer than the width of the bottom piece. The long 1x2 trim pieces are 1½ inches longer than the side pieces, and the short 1x2s are 4¼ inches long.

2. Build and brace.

Assemble the bottom and sides, drilling pilot holes and driving 2-inch deck screws to form a strong box. Add the 1x2 trim, which covers up the edges of the end and bottom pieces, flush to the bottom and top of the box. Fasten the trim with 4d galvanized nails. Cap the box off with 1x3 top trim, mitered at the corners and attached with 6d galvanized nails.

Apply paint or sealer. Anchor the box as described at left. Choose a decorative bracket like the one shown, or use a miter-cut 2x2 in the same way as the 4x4 angle brace is used on page 67. Fill with 2 inches of gravel, followed by light soil.

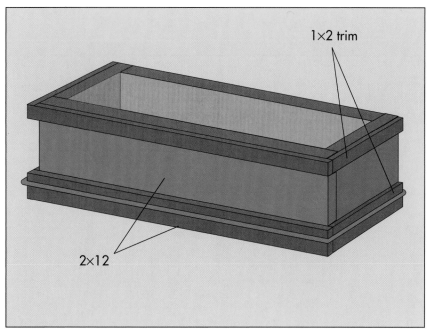

Building a large window box.

You can do some serious gardening outside your window with a massive box like this. Build it simply, using materials like pressure-treated 2×12 and painting it the color of the house. If you want, you can cover it with siding to match your house, or add a few pieces of trim.

Decide whether you will be gardening from inside your home or outside, and position the box for easy access. You don't want to have to climb a ladder every time you water or weed.

Make a wood support.

Support a heavy box at three points. Anchor a ledger for the rear of the box to rest on; attach angled braces to support the front of the box; and anchor the top of the box directly to the house, adding washers as spacers to allow room for airflow.

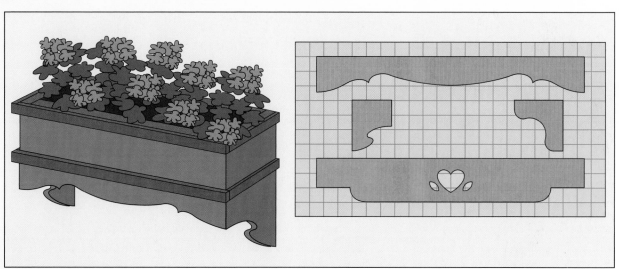

Add decorative touches.

Whether your window box is large or small, consider adding some ornamental touches. Make an apron like the one shown above, or come up with your own design, perhaps mirroring some other decorative element from your home's siding or trim.

You can make a cardboard template of half the design. Trace it onto a piece of 1× lumber, then flip it ove for the other half. Cut out carefully with a sabersaw. Sand all the curves so they look smooth. Attach the apron by drilling pilot and counterbore holes and driving screws upward.

Even if the box is otherwise supported, consider adding decorative end braces as well. Trace and cut them out of 1× lumber.

PLANNING SHEDS AND PLAY STRUCTURES

Although serviceable storage sheds and play structures can be purchased from any home center, if you build them yourself you can customize them to suit your site and your particular needs. If you are a reasonably skilled do-it-yourselfer with some basic skills and a willingness to plan the project carefully, you can build a shed or play structure. Check with your building department about how close to your property line you can build, what kind of foundation you must have, and the required sizes of the framing members.

RIGHT: *Utilitarian can be handsome. This shed incorporates decorative brackets and a row of clerestory windows for interior illumination.*

BELOW: *Play areas can be decorative as well as fun.*

RIGHT: *Playhouses can be as much fun to build as they are to play in, giving you a rare chance to have some fun with the materials at hand. This example is every bit a house in miniature. For a simpler design that can be built in a weekend, see pages 80–81.*

BELOW: *Instead of wading past the mower, wheelbarrow, and other large tools that gather in a tool shed, why not make shovels, rakes, and hoes readily accessible with this storage area? This shallow addition can be incorporated into a garage, potting shed, or storage shed.*

BELOW RIGHT: *For getting a jump on the planting season and gardening year-round, a greenhouse is a welcome addition. Although greenhouses are difficult to build from scratch, a wide variety of kits are available. See pages 74–75 for tips on how to put one together.*

BUILDING A FENCE-POST SHED

If you just want enclosed storage space but don't need a finished floor, this structure will do the trick—and for a small amount of labor and money. This building will fit into a narrow spot, yet have room for most gardening tools. You may want to use one-third of it to shelter garbage cans.

The basic structure uses 4×4 posts and 2×4 framing for easy construction. For the siding and the doors, choose regular 1×6, or buy tongue-and-groove 1×6 for a bit more strength and a more finished appearance.

The roof is raised above the main structure; therefore most, but not all, rainfall will be kept out. Corrugated fiberglass panels make a suitable roof, but if you want to install a regular shingle roof instead, see page 79.

As with most sheds, the roof framing will be the trickiest part to build. You will need a helper—an experienced carpenter will make the work go faster, but with patience you can build it with just another set of helping hands.

You can save construction time by using premade trusses. Check at the home center or lumberyard for trusses that will fit your project. Keep in mind that premade trusses cost more than site-built trusses.

Because all pieces will be exposed to the weather, use rot resistant lumber. T-hinges and large pulls for the doors are easy to install. For installing a latch, see page 31.

see page 79.

YOU'LL NEED

TIME: Two days, with a helper.
SKILLS: Basic measuring, leveling, cutting, and fastening.
TOOLS: Circular saw, drill, level, square, posthole digger.

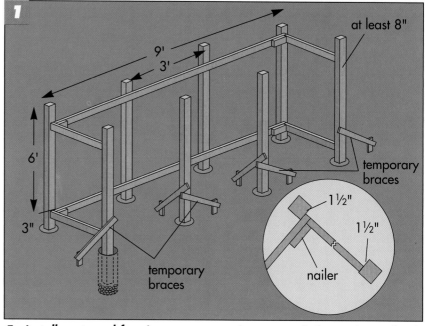

1. Install posts and framing.
Lay out for the posts, using stakes and string lines. Check for square (see page 13). Dig the postholes at least 30 inches deep or below the frost line. Shovel in a few inches of gravel, set the posts in the holes, and temporarily brace them plumb in both directions. Use a string line to line up the posts. Attach 2×4 pieces at top and bottom, as shown. Make sure all 2×4 pieces are level. Pour concrete and wait several days for it to cure.

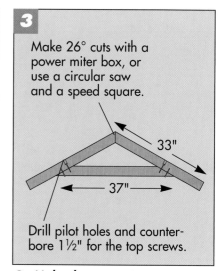

2. Add the siding.
Cut pieces of 1×6 to 72 inches, and attach them to the 2×4 framing pieces with 2-inch deck screws. (For tongue-and-groove, drive 6d galvanized nails through the tongues.) Because you are fitting boards between the posts, you will have to rip-cut pieces; see page 14.

3. Make the trusses.

Make 26° cuts with a power miter box, or use a circular saw and a speed square.

33"

37"

Drill pilot holes and counter-bore 1½" for the top screws.

3. Make the trusses.
Cut the posts to height, level with each other (see page 39). Assemble by drilling pilot holes and driving 3-inch screws. Build one truss, test it on a set of posts, disassemble, and use the pieces as templates for the other trusses.

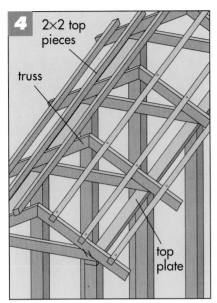

4. Attach top plates and trusses.

Cut two 2×4s to span the length of the shed, and attach them to the tops of the posts with 3-inch deck screws. Set the trusses directly above the posts, drill pilot holes, and angle-drive 3-inch deck screws to hold the trusses in place. They will be wobbly at this point, so work carefully. Attach 2×2 top pieces to the trusses, three on each side, evenly spaced.

5. Construct the roof.

Cut the fiberglass panels so they will overhang the lower end of the truss by an inch or so. Use a fine-toothed cutting blade on a circular saw. To save time and ensure that all the pieces will be the same length, stack three or four panels on top of each other and cut them all at once.

Lay panels on the roof, with pieces overlapping by one corrugation. Screw the panels to the top pieces by drilling pilot holes (to make sure you don't crack the fiberglass) and driving 2-inch screws that have washers and rubber gaskets to protect against leaks. Place the screws at the bottom of the corrugations, every 8 inches or so, and always drive screws where the sheets overlap. Cover the ridge with a cap made of two 1×4s.

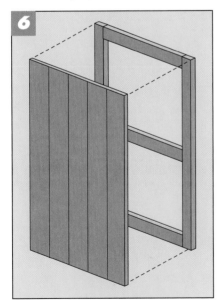

6. Build and hang the doors.

Measure your door openings and make doors to fit inside them. If an opening is not square (it happens to the best of carpenters), build the door to the larger dimensions, and then cut it to fit the nonsquare opening by sawing through the siding and framing at the same time. Build a simple frame out of 2×4s, connecting the pieces by drilling pilot holes and angle-driving 3-inch deck screws. It does not have to be strong. Lay it on a flat working area, and attach 1×6s in the same way as you did the siding. Support the door on blocks while you fasten the hinges. Add a door pull and a latch.

BUILDING A LEAN-TO SHED

A small shed like this has an advantage over a larger structure: It's not big enough to hold so many tools that you lose track of them. You can build a larger structure than shown on these pages, but make it longer, and not much wider, so that it will be easy to keep organized. If you make it wider by a foot or more, use 2×6s instead of 2×4s for the rafters and the floor joists.

Plan the size according to your needs. You may want to install a workbench or a potting bench. Be sure all your tools can be hung within easy reach, so you don't have to pile them up in a corner. If you want to do some carpentry work out of the shed, plan to store sawhorses in it, so you can quickly bring them outside. You may want to have an electrician install a receptacle.

If you live in an area with cold winters, frost heave will cause shallow footings to rise and fall as much as an inch. If your shed will be attached to the house, it is important that it not rise and fall while the house stays still. Either leave the shed unattached or check with local regulations; and be sure to dig and pour footings that extend below your frost line—the depth to which ground freezes during the winter.

Because the structure will be exposed to the weather, use pressure-treated lumber and plywood throughout.

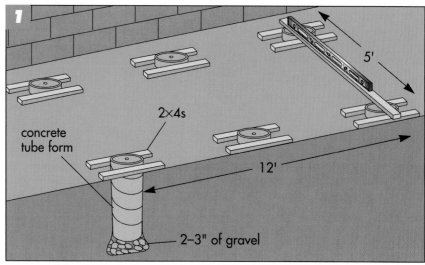

1. Install footings.
Mark the outline of your shed with stakes and string lines, and check for square (see page 13). Because the footing of a house is usually wider than its walls, you will probably not be able to dig right next to the house. Dig postholes below your frost line. Shovel 2 to 3 inches of gravel into each hole for drainage.

All the footings must be level with each other. Use a level and a straight board to find the highest spot, and start there. Insert a tube form and anchor it as shown, or use the arrangement shown on page 17. Then anchor all the other tube forms at the same level.

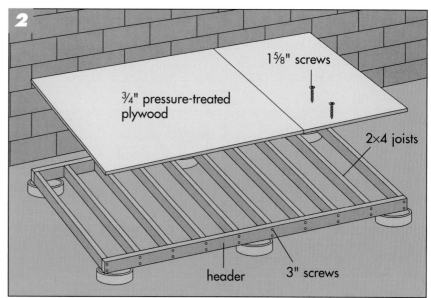

2. Build the floor.
Cut two 2×4 headers to the exact length of the shed, and cut the joists to its width, minus 3 inches. Work on a large, flat surface. Lay the headers side by side and mark them for joists every 16 inches (see page 77). Set all the pieces in place, and attach with two 3-inch deck screws at each joint. Set the floor frame on the concrete footings, and check for square.

Cut pieces of ¾-inch pressure-treated plywood to fit. Attach the plywood to the joists with 1⅝-inch deck screws.

3. Frame the shed.

Attach a ledger board to the house 8 feet above the floor. Make sure it is level and that the ends are plumb with the ends of the floor. Build the 7-foot-high front wall by laying it out on the floor. Raise it into position and temporarily brace it so it is plumb. To make the first rafter, have a helper hold a 2×4 in place while you mark it. Use it as a template for the others. Attach the rafters with angle-driven 2-inch decking screws. For the side walls, measure each stud individually by holding it in place with a level to make sure it is plumb while you mark it.

4. Build the roof.

Cut ½-inch plywood to fit, so it overhangs the rafters by 2 inches on all three sides. Attach with 1⅝-inch deck screws. Staple on roofing felt, and lay the shingles. Install flashing where the roof meets the house; consult with your supplier or inspector for the right installation on your house.

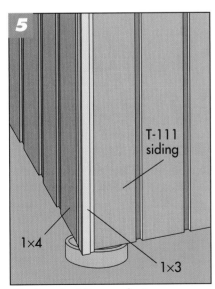

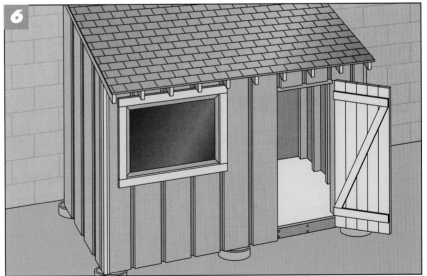

5. Attach siding and trim.

Cover the exterior of the shed with T-111 siding. Make it snug against the house, and keep it about 2 inches above the ground. Caulk the joint where the plywood meets the house, and trim the outside corners with pieces of 1×3 and 1×4 lumber.

6. Add window and door; paint.

To build a simple door, use the instructions for a Z-frame gate, pages 28–29. Make the door out of a piece of sheet siding or use 1×6s with no spaces between them. Attach to the shed with T-hinges, and add a door spring if you want it to close automatically.

Add a gate latch or install a hasp with a padlock for security (see page 31). Install your window, and trim it with butt-jointed 1×3s.

Apply two heavy coats of exterior paint to the siding, taking care to ensure that the bottom of each piece of lumber is well coated with paint.

ASSEMBLING A GREENHOUSE KIT

In areas with mild winters, a greenhouse can mean year-round flowers and vegetables. If your climate is more severe, it can lengthen the growing season so you can have fresh tomatoes and bright zinnias as early as May or as late as November.

You can grow plants to full maturity in large containers in a greenhouse, later moving them outdoors. Or use a greenhouse as you would a cold frame, starting seeds early so you can plant healthy seedlings outside as soon as spring arrives.

This freestanding greenhouse will be dependent on the sun for warmth. You can also build a greenhouse up against a house, and open a door or window to heat it when necessary. To receive the full benefit of the sun, orient your greenhouse toward the south. Be aware, however, that a greenhouse produces plenty of heat and humidity, and an attached model might make your home uncomfortably warm. Often venting the heat is as important a consideration as holding it.

Because it is difficult to build a watertight, glassed-in structure yourself, purchasing a greenhouse kit is a good idea. These steps will give you a general idea of how most kits are assembled.

YOU'LL NEED
TIME: With a helper, a day and a half to excavate, lay the timbers, and assemble a greenhouse kit.
SKILLS: Measuring, leveling, cutting, driving screws.
TOOLS: Shovel, circular saw, level, drill, tape measure, baby sledge.

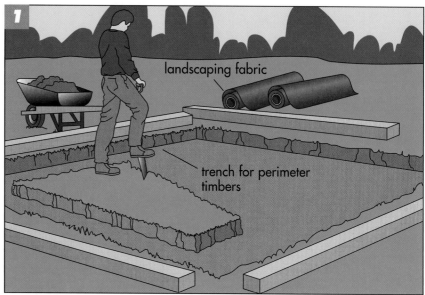

1. Lay out and excavate the bed.
Cut 4×6 landscaping timbers or railroad ties to the lengths required by your kit, and lay them in position at the site. Use the 3-4-5 method to check for square (page 13). Once positioned, use the timbers as a template; cut the perimeter with a shovel. Remove the timbers and dig away all the sod and other organic material in the area. Dig a trench for the timbers and fill it with 2 inches of gravel; you want the timbers to be about an inch above grade once they're placed. Lay landscaping fabric over the entire area (including the trench).

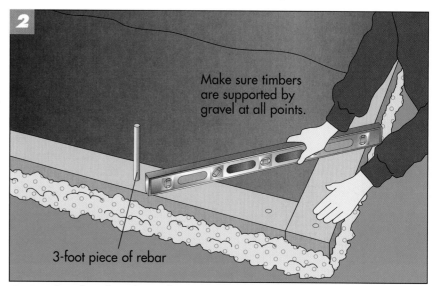

2. Level and anchor the timbers.
Set the timbers back in place, on top of the gravel, and check them for level. It will take some time for you to get them level and well supported with gravel.

Drill holes through the timbers every 16 inches or so, and drive 3-foot pieces of rebar or galvanized pipe down through each hole and into the ground.

Add enough pea gravel to fill in the floor so that it comes up to within about an inch of the tops of the timbers.

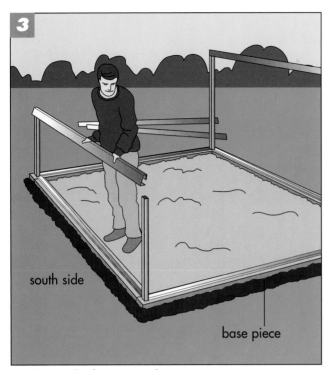

3. Screw the frames in place.

Chalk lines on the timbers indicating the exact perimeter of the greenhouse. Attach the base pieces to the timbers. Attach the corner uprights to the frame, then connect the horizontal rails. Once these are in, you can add the angled roof pieces and the top ridge. Work carefully—the structure will not be stable.

4. Attach panels to the frame.

Have a helper hold each acrylic panel in place while you insert the hold-down screws. For each sheet, first position all the screws, then tighten them down.

5. Install hinged vents.

Insert the hinged vents into the eave on the south side of the structure. The large clearance in the hinges should allow the panels to move smoothly up and down and from side to side. Connect the vent openers. Adjust the black cylinder by screwing it in or out so the vent opens at the desired temperature.

6. Seal the joints and plant seeds.

If called for, apply silicone caulk to the joints to ensure a tight seal. Most greenhouses are designed so that plants placed on benches at a good working height (about 30 inches) will get optimal sunlight. The north wall of the greenhouse reflects light back onto the plants.

BUILDING A SHED ON SKIDS

This shed is about as simple as a freestanding roofed structure can be. Unlike the fence-post shed on pages 72–73, this one is completely enclosed to keep things dry inside. Building on skids saves you the work of installing a foundation; the weight of the shed keeps it stable. You'll need to know the size of the rough openings so you'll be able to purchase your window and prehung door before you build. A suggested size for the shed is 8 feet by 12 feet.

YOU'LL NEED

TIME: Several weekends, with a skilled helper.
SKILLS: Basic carpentry.
TOOLS: Circular saw, handsaw, drill, shovel, level, T-bevel.

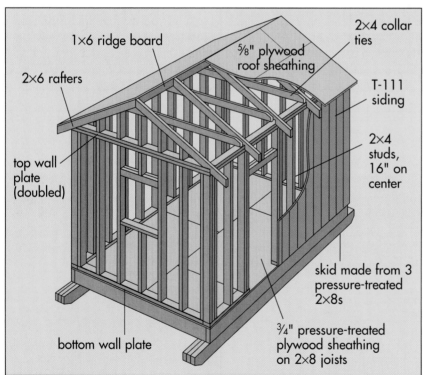

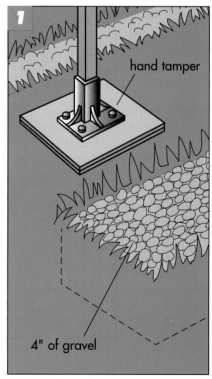

1. Provide a foundation.

Project overview.
The structure rests on massive skids made of triple 2×8s. The floor framing is made of 2×8 joists, 16 inches on center.

The shed uses standard stud construction with 2×4 studs 16 inches on center. The roof is supported by 2×6 rafters, 24 inches on center, that meet on a 1×6 ridge board at the peak. Collar ties on at least every other rafter ensure that the tops of the walls will not bow outward.

1. Provide a foundation.
The skids must be level with each other. Dig two parallel trenches, 3 feet longer than the shed's length, and fill the trenches with 4 inches of well-tamped gravel. Check that the tamped gravel is level.

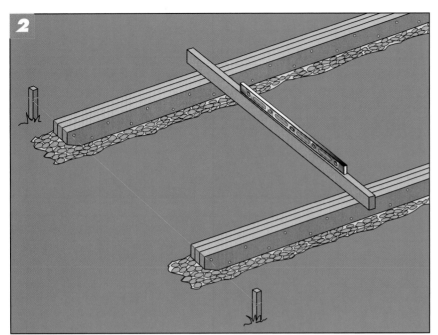

2. Build and set the skids.

Make the skids out of three pressure-treated 2×8s; be sure they have a cca retention level of at least .40 or a label that says *ground contact.*

Cut the first piece 32 inches longer than the length of the shed, giving it a decorative cut like the one shown. Use it as a template for the other five pieces. Laminate the pieces together with glue and by driving 3-inch deck screws in an alternating pattern every 6 inches.

Set the skids on the gravel. Run a string line that touches both ends, and use the 3-4-5 method to check for square (see page 13). Make sure the skids are level with the ground and level with each other.

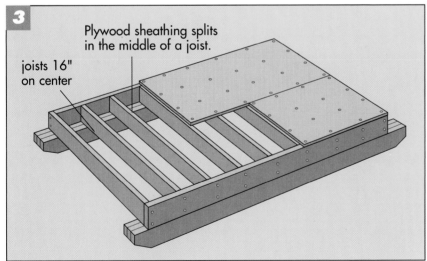

joists 16" on center

Plywood sheathing splits in the middle of a joist.

3. Frame and sheath the floor.

Use pressure-treated 2×8s and plywood. Cut two 2×8s to the length of your shed, set them next to each other, and mark for joists that are 16 inches on center. (This means that you must subtract ¾ inch from each multiple of 16 before making your line; see the drawing for step 4.)

Cut joists to the width of the shed, minus 3 inches, and assemble the framing box with 3-inch deck screws. Use the plywood to make sure the frame is square. Attach plywood to the joists with 1⅝-inch deck screws.

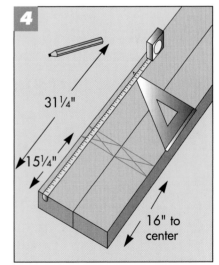

31¼"

15¼"

16" to center

4. Cut and lay out wall plates.

For each wall, begin by cutting the bottom and top plates. Set them next to each other, and lay them out as you did the floor joists. Study the framing drawing on page 78 before laying out for the window and door.

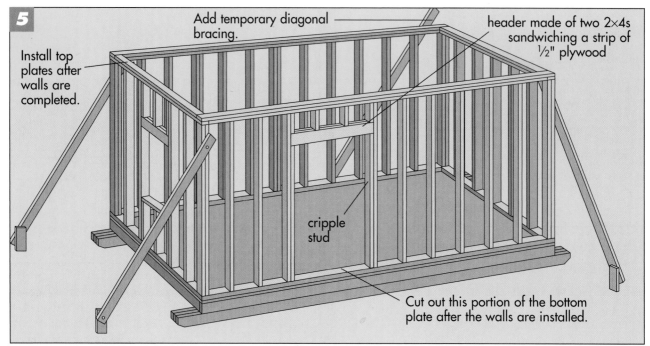

5

Install top plates after walls are completed.

Add temporary diagonal bracing.

header made of two 2×4s sandwiching a strip of ½" plywood

cripple stud

Cut out this portion of the bottom plate after the walls are installed.

5. Frame the walls.

Have your prehung door and your window on hand, so you know the rough openings for each. Buy precut studs, or cut them to the height of the wall, minus 4½ inches.

Note that on either side of the window and the door, cripple studs are used. Assemble the walls on the shed floor or another flat surface. Position the studs on the layout lines, and drive two 3-inch deck screws or

16d nails for each joint. With two or more helpers, raise each wall into position and temporarily brace it so it is plumb in both directions. Fasten the walls together and set the top plate to overlap the walls.

EXPERTS' INSIGHT

FIGURING ROOF PITCH

The horizontal distance traveled by a rafter is called the roof's run. The vertical distance, from the top of the wall to the top of the roof, is the rise. The slope of a roof is inches of rise per inches of run. A 6–12 pitch, for instance, means that the roof rises 6 inches for every 12 inches of run.

Check with your local building department for pitch requirements before building. You may want to duplicate the pitch of your house roof on your shed's roof. To figure the pitch of an existing roof, use two levels, one held plumb and the other held level, and measure the rise and run.

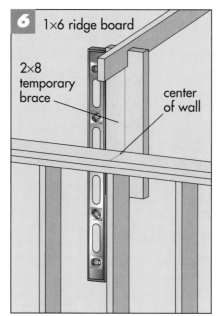

6

1×6 ridge board

2×8 temporary brace

center of wall

6. Temporarily prop the ridge.

Determine how high your ridge board should be. At each end, firmly anchor a notched piece of 2×8 to the inside of the wall framing. Use a level to make sure the board is plumb. Cut a 1×6 ridge board to the length of the shed, and set it in place.

7

birds-mouth cut

ridge cut

7. Mark for the rafters.

Have two helpers hold a 2×6 in place against the ridge board and the top plate while you mark with a pencil. Mark the top cut at the ridge and the birds-mouth cut where the rafter will sit on the top wall plate. You may have to experiment before getting it right.

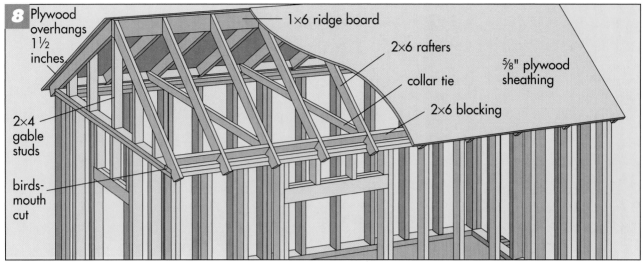

8 Plywood overhangs 1½ inches

1×6 ridge board

2×6 rafters

collar tie

⅝" plywood sheathing

2×6 blocking

2×4 gable studs

birds-mouth cut

8. Build the roof.

This will be the most time-consuming part of the job. Cut two rafters and test them by holding them in place; the joints at the ridge and at the top plate should be tight. Use the first rafter as a template for making the others. Cut 2×6 blocking pieces to 22½ inches so that you will end up with rafters spaced 24 inches on center.

Work with at least two helpers because your structure will be very wobbly at first. Mark layout lines on the top plates and both sides of the ridge. Have the helpers hold the rafters in place as you attach. Drive nails through the ridge and into the rafters, and toenail at the birds-mouth cut. Install the blocking as you go. Every other rafter, install a collar tie. Cut and notch 2×4 gable studs to fit.

Attach the plywood sheathing with 8d nails. Let it overhang the gable ends by 1½ inches. Immediately cover the sheathing with roofing material.

9

⅛" gap

9. Install window and siding.

Attach the window to the framing; check for plumb and square before driving screws. Add Z flashing above the door. Then attach ⅝-inch T-111 siding directly to the studs with 8d siding nails, 6 inches apart on the edges and 12 inches apart elsewhere. Leave a ⅛-inch gap between the siding and the window frame, and caulk it. Trim the corners with 1×3 and 1×4 (see page 73).

10

Plumb and attach hinge side first.

jamb

10. Install a prehung door.

Buy a solid-core exterior door with a lockset that will withstand inclement weather. Attach the hinge side of the jamb first, checking for plumb and driving 8d casing nails. Make the front edge of the jamb flush with the siding. Shim and attach the other side of the jamb so the door closes easily. Attach brick molding over the jamb and siding.

11

ledger

2×4 frame

11. Add a landing.

Start with a ledger board attached to the shed, and support the front of the 2×4 frame with posts sunk in concrete or tamped soil. To keep rain and snow out of the shed, make sure that the top of the finished landing will be an inch or so below the interior floor and tilted slightly to the outside.

BUILDING A SIMPLE PLAYHOUSE

Some playhouses are grand productions that use the same construction techniques you might expect in a full-size house, including stud walls, rafters, and real windows and doors—sometimes even electrical wiring. However, given that kids typically outgrow a playhouse in a few years, it makes sense to keep things simple. This project can be built in a weekend. Because it uses plywood reinforced with minimal framing, the only difficult steps involve plunge-cutting the windows and doors.

YOU'LL NEED

TIME: Two days, with a helper.
SKILLS: Basic carpentry, applying roof shingles.
TOOLS: Circular saw, level, hammer, handsaw, tape measure, drill, chalk line.

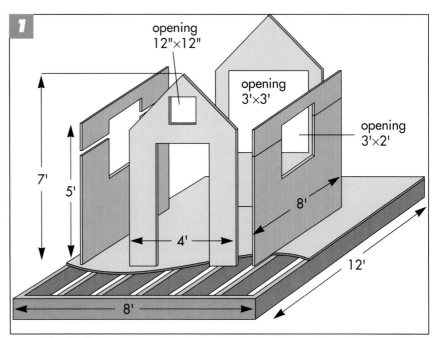

opening 12"×12"
opening 3'×3'
opening 3'×2'
7'
5'
4'
8'
12'
8'

1. Make the base.
Using pressure-treated 2×4s, build a framing box for the floor. Make it larger than the house will be (see step 6), with joists 16 or 24 inches on center. Sheath the frame with ½-inch pressure-treated plywood. (See pages 72 and 77 for instructions on laying out joists and building a base.)

Support the plywood well so ends of cuts do not crack.

2. Cut the pieces.
Mark a chalk line on a sheet of ¾-inch plywood and cut the perimeter of the front piece as shown in step 1. Use it as a template for the rear piece. For each of the sides, use one full sheet and one sheet rip-cut to 12 inches wide (see page 14).

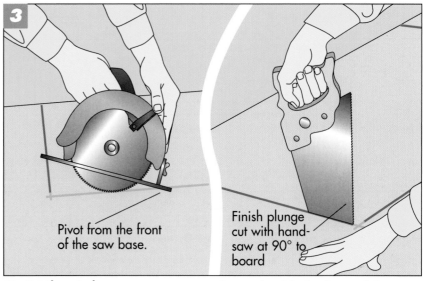

Pivot from the front of the saw base.

Finish plunge cut with handsaw at 90° to board

3. Cut the windows.
Place the top and bottom wall pieces together and mark the window opening. Measure and mark the end windows. Cut out with a circular saw. You will need to make some plunge cuts. Set the blade to the correct depth. Retract the safety guard and tilt the saw

forward, with the front of the baseplate resting on the plywood. Start the saw and lower it slowly into the cut line.

Finish the cuts with a handsaw, held at a 90-degree angle to the plywood so it cuts the same distance on both sides.

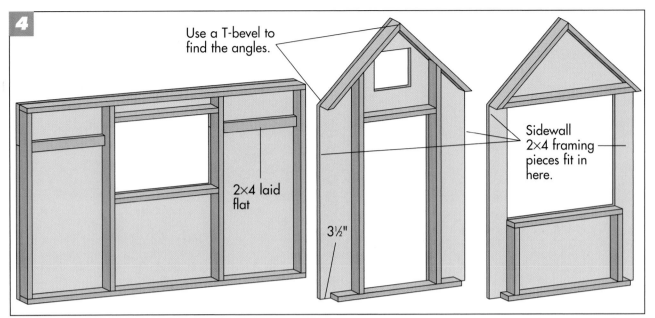

4

Use a T-bevel to find the angles.

2×4 laid flat

3½"

Sidewall 2×4 framing pieces fit in here.

4. Add framing and assemble.

Reinforce the plywood walls with 2×4 frames. For each of the side walls, build a rectangular box, the same size as the wall, out of four 2×4s fastened together with 3-inch deck screws. Lay the plywood on top, and fasten with 2-inch deck screws. Turn the wall over and add 2×4s to frame around the window, and flat-laid 2×4s to secure the plywood splice.

With two helpers, raise one end wall and one side wall, and attach them at each corner with 2-inch screws driven through the end wall and into the framing of the side wall.

Add framing for the end walls as shown. Use a T-bevel to find the angles, and cut the pieces with a circular saw. Attach the end walls to the side walls with 3-inch screws tying 2×4s together and 2-inch screws driven through the plywood.

Center the structure on the base, and attach it with 3-inch screws driven into joists.

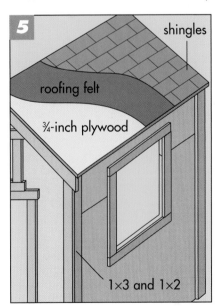

5

shingles

roofing felt

¾-inch plywood

1×3 and 1×2

5. Add the trim and the roof.

Trim is not necessary, but it will make the structure look more like a real house. For something easy to install yet charming, use butt-jointed 1×3s as shown. Install ¾-inch plywood for the roof, and lay roofing felt and shingles.

6

6. Decorate and paint.

Trim and decorate to suit your kids' taste. See pages 96–99 for ideas on shutters. Adding a simple 2×4 fence around the "deck" like the one shown here is a nice finishing touch and makes your kids feel like real homeowners.

Sand all the edges well so there will be no splinters. Brush on two coats of high-quality exterior paint—bright, primary colors are a good choice.

INSTALLING A PLAYGROUND AREA

*I*f you can find a playground kit to suit your kids' requirements that is made of high-quality materials, you'll likely pay a high price. You may, however, be able to buy the components your kids enjoy most and build from your own design at a more modest cost.

Use lumber that won't rot and is unlikely to splinter. Heartwood of redwood or cedar is a good choice. Pressure-treated lumber is not dangerous after it is installed but it may crack. Kiln-dried pressure-treated wood (KDAT) is less likely to splinter, and is worth the expense.

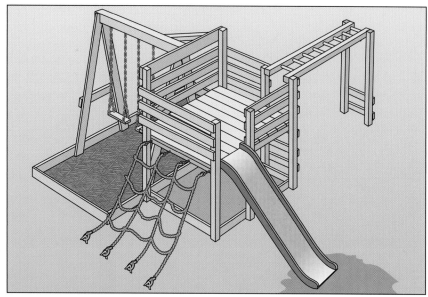

YOU'LL NEED

TIME: Two days, with a helper.
SKILLS: Measuring, plumbing and leveling, cutting.
TOOLS: Level, circular saw, wrenches, posthole digger, drill.

This playground area has features for children in several age groups. A semisheltered sandbox provides a place for toddlers to play. Swings, a slide, a net ladder, and a platform keep young chldren

happy and active. And hand-over-hand bars add a challenge for older kids. Whatever features you include, keep in mind how tough kids can be when they're playing, and build accordingly.

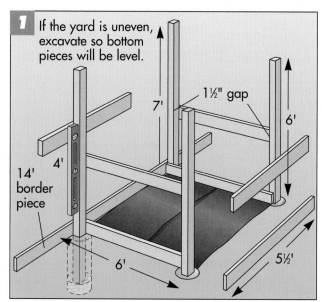

1. Build the basic frame.
Lay out for four postholes that form a square (see page 13), dig them at least 30 inches deep, and shovel in a few inches of gravel. Excavate away all the sod from the area inside the square, and cover the area with landscaping fabric.

Place the posts and temporarily brace two of them so they are plumb in both directions. Construct the frame as shown, out of 4×4s and 2×6s. Drive two 3-inch screws at each joint. Cut the posts to height.

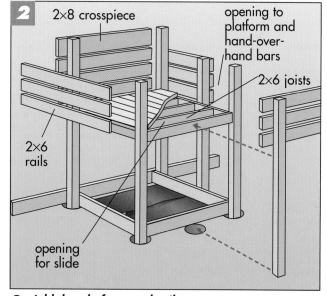

2. Add the platform and rails.
Install three evenly spaced 2×6 interior joists. Cut and fasten decking boards (either 2×6s or 5/4 × 6 decking), leaving a 1/4-inch gap between the boards. Install two more posts, leaving room for the hand-over-hand bars on one side and the ladder on the other. Cut and install 2×6 rails and one 2×8 crosspiece, spacing them evenly and checking for level.

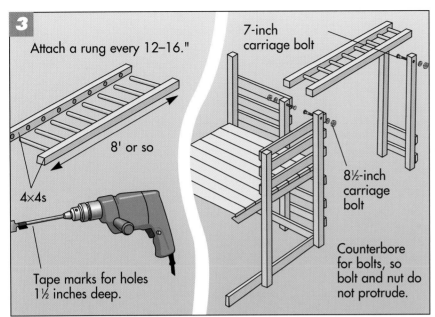

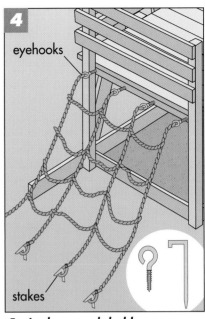

3. Make the hand-over-hand bars.
Place a piece of tape on a 1¼-inch drill bit as a depth gauge for boring holes 1½ inches deep. Cut two 4×4s to the length of the hand-over-hand bars, lay them side by side, and mark them both for evenly spaced holes. Drill the holes. Cut 1¼-inch dowel pieces that are 4 inches shorter than the total width of the bars. Dry-fit the pieces to make sure the unit will fit snugly in your opening. Disassemble, squirt polyurethane glue into each hole, reassemble, and clamp together. Install two posts at the other end of the hand-over-hand bars.

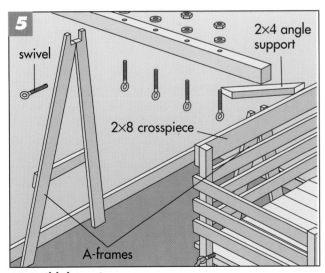

4. Anchor a web ladder.
Where the ladder will attach to the platform, drill holes and install eyehooks. Attach the ladder to the hooks; you may need to open the hooks and close them with tongue-and-groove pliers. Attach the web or rope ladder to the ground by driving stakes.

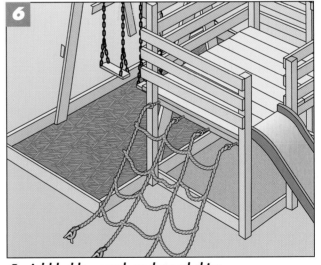

5. Build the swing set.
On a 12-foot-long 4×6 or 4×8 beam, mark for holes, depending on the width of your swing seats. Drill with a long bit, and install eyehooks for the swings. Construct A-frames out of 2×6s, with notches at the top so the beam will fit snugly. Attach one A-frame to the 2×8 crosspiece, set the beam in its notch, and have a helper hold the other A-frame while you set the beam into its notch. Add the 2×4 angle support, driving 3-inch screws to secure the beam.

6. Add ladder, sand, and wood chips.
Add the three remaining framing pieces under the swing set area, excavate the area, and install landscaping fabric. Fill this area with wood chips, and fill the area under the platform with sand. (To keep the neighborhood cats from using this area as a litter box, cover the sand with a tarp at night.) Attach the ladder and the swings according to manufacturer's directions. Sand the structure carefully, and paint or apply finish.

DESIGNING DECORATIVE IMPROVEMENTS

Some projects are just plain fun to build. Whether you add a set of shutters to dress up your home or a perky cupola to your garage, or simply build a fancifully painted birdhouse for the backyard, these decorative elements are a chance to add personality to your home and landscape.

Many of the projects shown on the following pages can be built in a couple of hours and involve even the youngest member of the family. All start with basic designs that you can customize to suit your site.

RIGHT: *Long a folk art tradition in which the builder gives free reign to his or her imagination, whimsical birdhouses make an eye-catching display when congregated in a miniature village.*

LEFT: *A garden pond requires some planning and maintenance to keep the fish flourishing, the water clear, and the plants healthy. But a refreshing oasis like this is well worth the effort. See pages 102–105.*

BELOW: *Pretty as a flower, some birdhouses may never attract a bird but can be a delightful addition to your yard.*

ABOVE: *Design functional birdhouses to suit the type of bird you want to attract (see pages 90–91).*

RIGHT: *Shutters are a quick way to dress up windows and add color to your house (see pages 96–99).*

BELOW: *A bridge over a dry creek divides space and adds a fantasy dimension (see pages 100–101).*

MAKING AND INSTALLING A CUPOLA

A small cupola on the top of your garage or garden shed is fun to build and makes a big impact. It is an ideal location for a weather vane (see page 89), and you can add louvered vents or a built-in birdhouse. Trim and siding can be varied to harmonize with that of your garage or shed.

Though these structures can be adjusted in scale to suit your location, keep in mind that it is far easier to build a cupola on the ground and position it later, rather than building it on the roof. Make it too large and you'll have difficulty getting it on the roof. Use high-quality rot resistant wood, such as clear redwood. Caulk your cupola so it is tightly sealed, and give it at least two generous coats of paint or sealer.

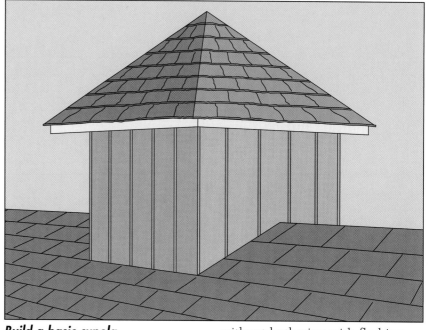

Build a basic cupola.
This cupola is the right size for most one- or two-car garages. Add it to a garage with a finished roof in good condition. To install it, attach nailers to the roof, then attach the cupola to the nailers. That way, you can eliminate leaks without bothering with flashing.

The vertical siding shown is just one option; feel free to cover your cupola with beveled siding or plywood. It often works best to make the cupola look like a miniature house, so mimic your garage's siding on a smaller scale.

YOU'LL NEED

TIME: Most of a day to build and install a cupola.
SKILLS: Careful measuring and cutting, attaching with screws, working on a roof.
TOOLS: Power miter saw or hand miter box, circular saw, drill, level, speed square.

CAUTION!
SAFETY WHILE WORKING ON A ROOF
Though you will not be doing anything complicated up there, take special care while working on a roof. Have a stable ladder resting against the eaves, and make sure someone is close by, in case you get into trouble. If your roof is steeply pitched, install ladder jacks (available at rental centers) or hire a professional roofer.

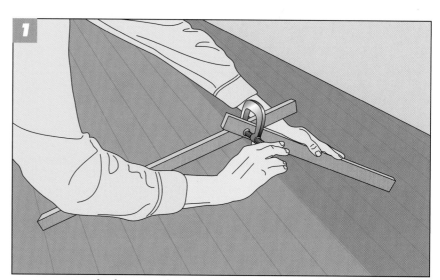

1. Determine the base angles.
Rather than going to the trouble of computing your roof's pitch and then transferring the calculation to the cupola's base, use this simple technique. Go up on the roof with two pieces of straight 1×2, each about 16 inches long, and a C-clamp. At the future location of the cupola, lay the 1×2s on the roof so they cross each other, and clamp them tight, so they will not fall out of alignment as you work.

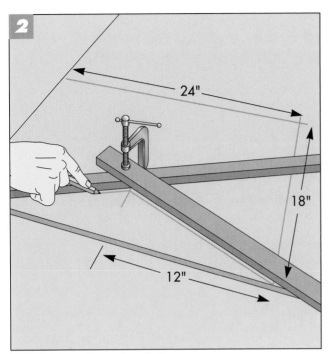

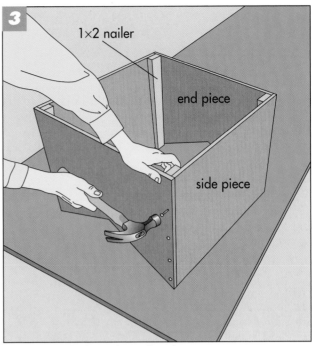

2. Cut the side and end pieces.

On a piece of ¾-inch pressure-treated plywood, use a framing square to mark four pieces 18 inches high and 24 inches long. Cut the four pieces. On two of the pieces, position the clamped 1×2s and mark for the roof line; be sure the peak is in the center. Use the first end piece as a template for the second.

3. Assemble the side and end pieces.

Cut four 1×2 nailers to 17 inches and attach them to the side pieces with their tops and sides flush with the top and side edges of the side pieces. Use 1¼-inch decking screws or 4d galvanized nails. Attach the end pieces by driving screws or nails into the 1×2s.

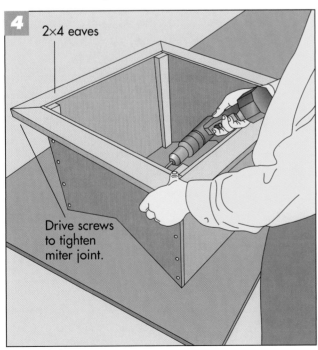

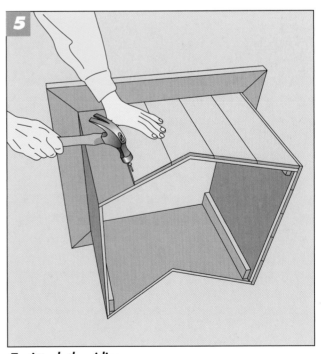

4. Add the eaves.

With a hand or power miter saw, miter-cut pieces of 2×4, so that the short side is the width of the cupola. Attach to the cupola by driving 1⅝-inch deck screws from inside the cupola. Tighten the joints by driving screws through the sides of the 2×4s as well.

5. Attach the siding.

Cut pieces of siding and attach them with 4d galvanized siding nails. You may cut them first, as shown, or install them a little long so they overhang the cutout for the peak of the roof, and then cut all the extra length off at once.

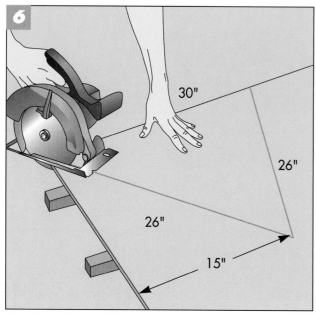

6. Cut roof sheathing.

On a piece of ¾-inch plywood, mark for a triangle, 30 inches at the base and 26 inches along the sides. To ensure that the peak is in the center, measure in 15 inches from the side, as shown. Cut, and use this form as a template for three more triangles. Cut four pieces of 1×2 to 22 inches. On two of the plywood triangles, attach a 1×2 flush to the edge of each 26-inch side, allowing 2 inches of space at each corner.

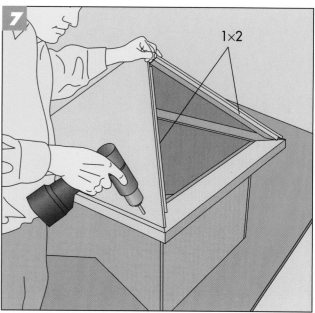

7. Construct the roof.

Attach the pieces with 1⅝-inch deck screws. Have a helper hold one of the triangles with 1×2s on one side, while you hold the other. Position them so they meet at the peak, and the plane of the plywood is flush with the edge of the eave. Drive 1⅝-inch decking screws at an angle at the bottom of each piece. Fasten the other two triangles with screws driven into the 1×2s.

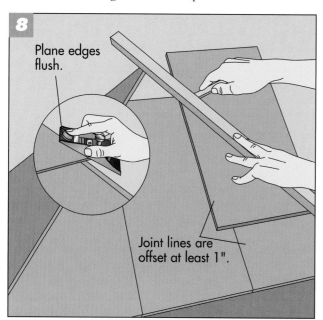

8. Finish the roof.

Cut standard shingles in half along their length, and use the thinner halves. Start at the bottom and work up. Make sure that the joint lines of each successive course are offset by at least an inch. Set each piece in place and mark it for cutting by using a straightedge. Install with 3d galvanized nails, hiding as many nails as possible. Use a plane to make the edges flush.

9. Install the cupola.

Carry the cupola to the roof, and find the best-looking location by viewing from below. To install it, attach four 2×4 nailers to the roof peak with 3-inch decking screws. Position them so the cupola just fits over them. Set the cupola in place, and attach it to the nailers by driving decking screws.

MAKING A WEATHER VANE

This old-fashioned feature is an ideal way to top off a cupola, garage, or shed. Originally, it had a practical use: Wind tends to swirl around buildings, so from the ground it can be difficult to tell which way it is blowing. On top of a roof, a weather vane gives a more accurate reading. Use materials that will not rust: Copper and stainless steel are good choices. Some vanes have directional indicators attached to horizontal poles—but these are not essential.

YOU'LL NEED

TIME: Several hours, depending on the complexity of the vane.
SKILLS: Cutting a pattern out of the material of your choice.
TOOLS: Sabersaw, tin snips, rod saw, pliers or wrenches.

1. Choose or make a pattern.
Here are some classic shapes. Make sure the weather vane is not mounted symmetrically on the rod. The rod should be mounted at a point about one-third of the distance across the form. The wind will point the vane in the direction of the larger side.

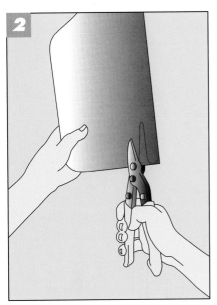

2. Cut the vane.
Heavy-gauge sheet metal will be a bit difficult to cut, but it has plenty of strength for its weight. Use tin snips if you can for at least some of the cuts. If you find you cannot cut curves with snips, equip a hacksaw with a rod saw blade, or use a sabersaw with a metal-cutting blade.

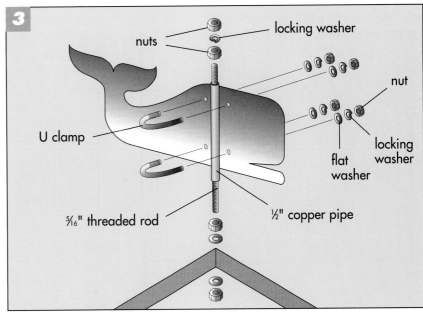

nuts — locking washer

nut

U clamp

flat washer / locking washer

$\frac{5}{16}$" threaded rod

$\frac{1}{2}$" copper pipe

3. Make a rotating stand.
Cut a piece of ½-inch copper pipe (rigid pipe, not copper tubing) that is as high as you want your vane to be above the cupola, and a length of 5/16-inch threaded rod that is several inches longer. Drill holes in the vane and attach it to the pipe with U-clamps, nuts, and washers. At the top of the rod, sandwich two nuts together around a locking washer.

Drill a 5/16-inch hole through the peak of the cupola. Thread one nut onto the bottom of the threaded rod, so that the copper pipe has about half an inch of play. Add a washer, insert the rod down through the roof, and tighten with another washer and nut inside the cupola. The vane should spin easily.

BUILDING BIRDHOUSES

Birds are not only fun to have around, they help keep your yard free of insects. In urban and suburban areas, however, birds have a difficult time finding a place to nest. A birdhouse may be the key to making your area a suitable habitat for certain types of birds. A bird feeder (pages 92–93) might also help.

Some birdhouses are purely decorative. So if you want to attract birds, design your project with specific inhabitants in mind (see chart below). Once it is built, don't paint it with bright colors; most birds prefer to blend in with their surroundings—green or brown tones are best—or apply a light stain to cedar or redwood.

Place a birdhouse where squirrels and cats can't get at it. To keep the inside dry, face the hole away from prevailing winds. If you hang the birdhouse, use two wires so it will not spin. Many birds are comfortable living fairly close to humans, but will get skittish when people approach. So place the house within easy viewing distance while keeping it away from often-used footpaths. Often the best option is to place the birdhouse on top of a pole made of pipe (see page 94).

Clean your birdhouse thoroughly once a year. Use a mildewcide if there is evidence of lice or other pests. Some birds will not move into a house that has not been cleaned.

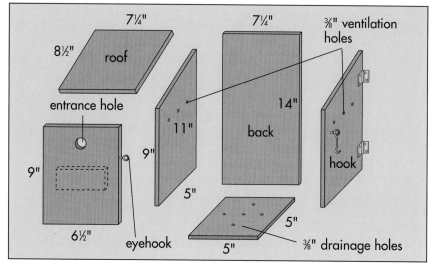

Plan a basic birdhouse.
Use this plan for a general-purpose birdhouse. Or decide which species of bird you want to attract, and build the house to the dimensions shown in the chart below. As you measure for cutting individual pieces, keep in mind how the pieces will overlap. For instance, the front piece should be 1½ inches wider than the floor.

Use cedar or redwood 1×8 lumber that is completely dry. Cut the pieces and drill the holes. Attach the nonhinged side, the floor, and the front together, drilling pilot holes and driving 1⅝-inch deck screws or 6d galvanized nails. Attach the other side with hinges only, and add the roof. Drill pilot holes and screw in the eye and the hook.

MATCHING THE HOUSE TO THE BIRD

Species	Floor Size	Height	Hole Diameter	Distance Above Ground
Bluebird	5" × 5"	8"	1½"	5' to 10'
Chickadee	4" × 4"	8" to 10"	1⅛"	6' to 15'
Finch	6" × 6"	6"	2"	8' to 12'
Flicker	7" × 7"	16" to 18"	2½"	6' to 20'
Kestrel or Screech Owl	8" × 8"	12" to 15"	3"	10' to 20'
Nuthatch	4" × 4"	8" to 10"	1¼"	12' to 20'
Starling	6" × 6"	16" to 18"	2"	10' to 25'
Tree Swallow	5" × 5"	6"	1½"	10' to 15'
Titmouse	4" × 4"	8" to 10"	1¼"	6' to 15'
Downy Woodpecker	4" × 4"	8" to 10"	1¼"	6' to 20'
Red-Bellied and Red-Headed Woodpecker	6" × 6"	12" to 15"	2½"	12' to 20'
Carolina Wren	4" × 4"	6" to 8"	1½"	6' to 10'
House Wren or Winter Wren	4" × 4"	6" to 8"	1" to 1¼"	6' to 10'

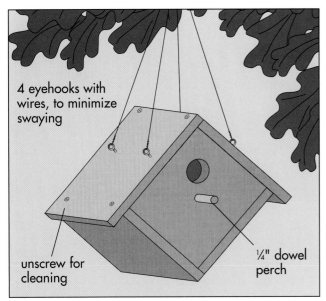

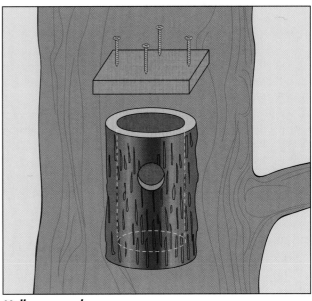

Build a diamond-shaped house with perch.

To build this simple project, cut front and back pieces about 8 inches square. Cut the side pieces to fit. The roof pieces should overhang the sides by about an inch. Use screws for at least one of the roof pieces, so you can remove it for cleaning. For the perch, drill a ¼-inch hole, squirt in a little polyurethane glue, and tap in a piece of ¼-inch hardwood dowel.

Hollow out a log.

This may last only a few years, but it is attractive and easy to build. Cut a piece of log that is about 4 inches thicker than the floor dimension you want (see the chart, page 90). Drilling from the top, make a series of holes with a 1-inch bit. (Mark the bit with a piece of tape, to make sure you don't drill too deeply.) Clean out the center with a chisel, and drill the opening hole. Attach the cover with screws.

Construct an open-ended house.

Robins, phoebes, and barn swallows will be attracted to a house with an open front. Place it 8 to 15 feet above the ground, securely anchored to a bough or trunk that will not sway in the wind. Position the house so it is at least partially protected from prevailing wind. There's no need for a hinged or removable section because you can clean this one easily.

Cut the sides, roof pieces, and floor out of 1×8 (which is actually 7¼ inches wide). You will need to bevel-cut the top edges of the side pieces at 45 degrees. Attach the pieces together with 2-inch deck screws or 6d galvanized nails. Add the 1×2 threshold and the mounting board, which doubles as the back of the house.

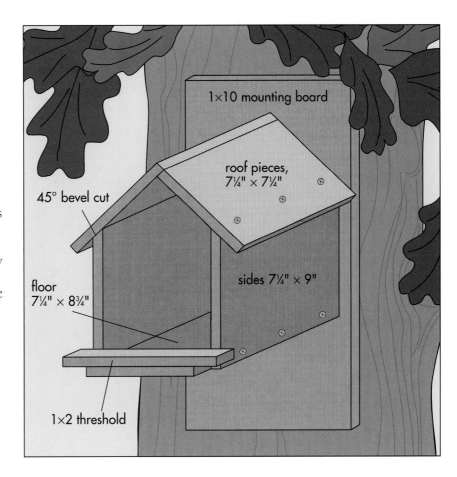

CONSTRUCTING BIRD FEEDERS

Because some birds are more sensitive than others to the presence of people, you may want to place two or three feeders at varying distances from the house. Experiment with different kinds of seed to find the type that attracts the birds you most want to see. If a feeder is close to a tree or some other form of cover rather than being out in the open, you will be more likely to attract shy birds. Make and place the feeder so it will be easy to fill.

YOU'LL NEED
TIME: Several hours.
SKILLS: Measuring, squaring, and cutting, driving nails or screws.
TOOLS: Saw, drill, square, hammer.

1. To make a hopper feeder, cut and assemble the pieces.
Use cedar or redwood 1×10 with very few knots. Cut the pieces to the dimensions shown. To make the cleats that hold the glass, rip-cut 1× stock to ¾ inch wide; the length does not have to be exact. Attach the cleats with small brads and polyurethane glue. Note the small piece at the bottom, to keep the glass from sliding down.

For all joints, drill pilot holes before driving 1⅝-inch decking screws or 6d galvanized nails. Assemble the back, sides, and floor. Add the 1×2 trim pieces, flush with the bottom so they form a lip for the tray. Attach the roof with hinges; make it so you can open it all the way for easy filling.

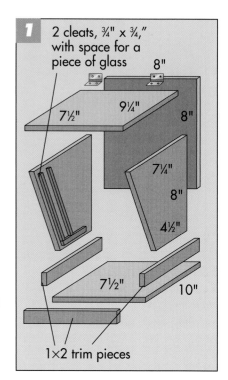

1 | 2 cleats, ¾" x ¾," with space for a piece of glass | 8" | 9¼" | 7½" | 8" | 7¼" | 8" | 4½" | 7½" | 10" | 1×2 trim pieces

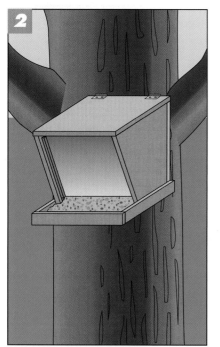

2. Add glass and mount.
Measure the opening and have a piece of glass cut to fit. Slide it into place; there's no need to caulk it. Attach the feeder to a pole or the side of a tree. Drill pilot holes and drive screws through the back or the bottom.

EXPERTS' INSIGHT

KEEPING THE SQUIRRELS AWAY
Squirrels are remarkably ingenious creatures. If there is a way for them to get at a feeder or a birdhouse, they will figure it out. So make a serious effort to outsmart them.

If you can hang a feeder by 2 feet or so of wire, that will probably keep them away. Or put the feeder on a pole and wrap the pole with 3 feet of galvanized or aluminum sheet metal; they will have a hard time climbing it.

You can buy ready-made baffles designed to keep squirrels from climbing a pole. Or make your own, using galvanized or aluminum sheet metal as shown.

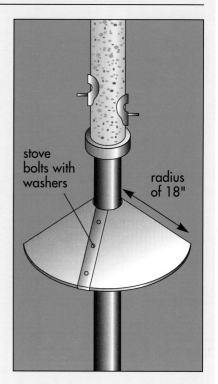

stove bolts with washers

radius of 18"

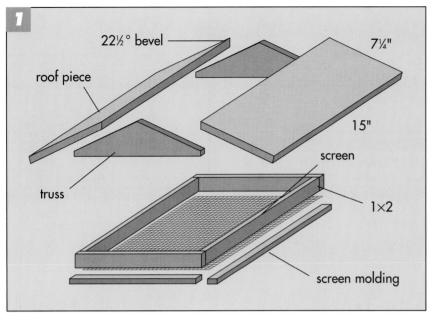

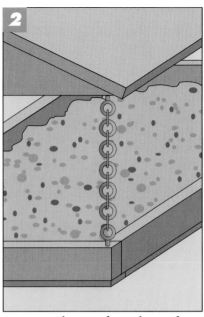

1. To make an open-air feeder, build the roof and the tray.

Use heartwood of redwood or cedar, clear or with only tiny knots. For all joints, drill pilot holes and drive 1⅝-inch screws or 6d galvanized nails.

Bevel-cut the top edge of the roof pieces at 22½ degrees. Temporarily join the roof pieces at the peak with small brads, and use the roof as a template to mark for the trusses. Cut the trusses and attach the roof to them.

Construct a 1×2 frame that will hang directly below the trusses. Cut aluminum screen to fit, and attach it to the underside with pieces of screen molding; attach the molding with small brads.

2. Hang the tray from the roof.

Insert four eyehooks into the trusses and four into the tray; position them so that the tray will hang directly below the roof. Cut four sections of chain, all with the same number of links, about 6 inches long. Use pliers to open the chain links, insert them into the eyehooks, and close them again.

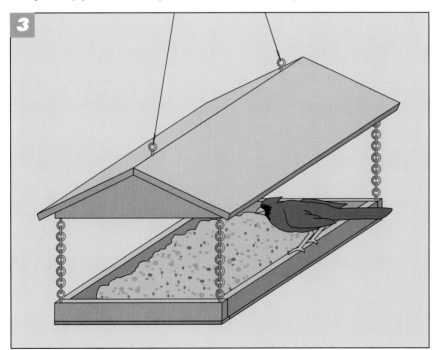

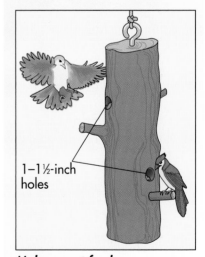

3. Finish and hang the feeder.

A coat of sealer/preservative will hold the natural color of your wood—otherwise it will turn gray. Insert two eyehooks through the peak of the roof. Hang the feeder with chain or wire. This feeder will be easy to load with seed, and the screen will help seeds to dry out after rains.

Make a suet feeder.

Some birds need suet to survive the winter. Although you can buy a hanging wire basket designed to hold suet, a section of log with holes bored in it works as well and blends better into the surroundings.

INSTALLING A FLORA AND FAUNA POLE

Here's a simple way to make your yard more interesting and fun: Install this knickknack shelf for the out-of-doors. Use it to hold two or three birdhouses, a bird feeder or two, plus a couple of potted plants. Interchangeability makes it handy: Showcase the flowerpots with the showiest bloom; experiment with birdhouses and a bath to see which birds can live together peacefully; fill feeders with different types of seeds to attract a variety of avian life. The pole is ideal for small yards, but can also make a focal point for a larger yard.

A utility pole or a cedar fence pole will be attractive; but a 6×6 post could be just as attractive, especially if you install dowels pointing in different directions. You could use a section of trunk from a recently felled tree, but don't expect it to last more than a few years.

YOU'LL NEED

TIME: Most of a day to build and install.
SKILLS: Cutting and anchoring a large pole, drilling holes, driving screws.
TOOLS: Drill, posthole digger, hammer, level.

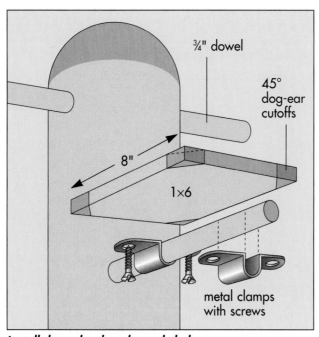

Install the pole, dowels, and shelves.
Dig a posthole at least 30 inches deep, shovel in a few inches of gravel, and insert the pole. Check for plumb in both directions, and temporarily brace the pole. Pour concrete, or firmly tamp soil into the hole. Mound the dirt or concrete up a bit, so rain water will run away from the pole.

At various points and facing different directions, drill

¾-inch holes into the pole. Keep the drill fairly level as you work. Cut ¾-inch dowels to extend out about 8 inches, apply a little polyurethane glue into the hold, and tap the dowels into place. Make the shelves by cutting a 1×6 to 8 inches, then making 45-degree dog-ear cuts on the corners; use the first shelf as a template for the others. After the glue on the dowels has set, attach the shelves with metal clamps and screws.

MAKING A BUTTERFLY HOUSE

Butterflies make your garden come alive with fresh colors. Though it may look like an unlikely residence, this butterfly house really does attract the fanciful creatures.

You don't want the house to stand out in the yard, so don't paint it bright colors. Brown or green tones that blend in with the setting will work well. Better yet, use cedar and give it a coat of sealer. This structure has a copper roof, but cedar would work just fine. Anchor the house firmly, so it does not sway in the wind. Use a pole (below), or attach it to a tree. The butterfly house will attract more butterflies if it is surrounded by foliage than attached to a house.

YOU'LL NEED

TIME: Several hours to build and install.
SKILLS: Accurate cutting of small slits, attaching with screws or nails, anchoring a pole in the ground.
TOOLS: Drill, posthole digger, hammer, level, circular saw, sabersaw with fine-cutting blade.

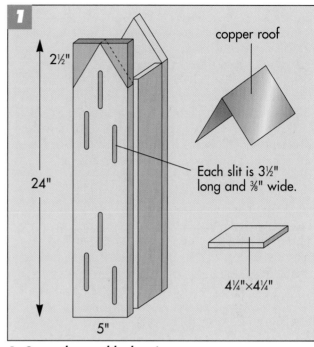

1. Cut and assemble the pieces.
Cut pieces to the dimensions shown. The tricky part is making slits. Draw lines carefully, using a square. Drill one or two ⅜-inch holes at each end of a slit, and cut the middle with a sabersaw equipped with a fine-cutting blade. Cut a piece of copper sheet metal with tin snips, and use a straightedge to bend it.

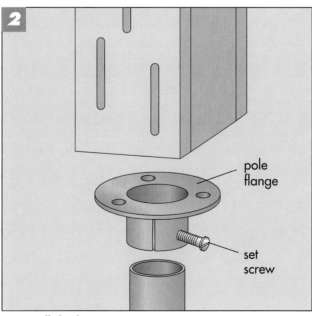

2. Install the house.
Drive an aluminum pole into the ground to anchor it. Attach a pole flange to the underside of the house by drilling pilot holes and driving screws. Slip the flange onto the pole and tighten the set screw.

3. Plant butterfly-attracting plants.
Surround the house with flowers that butterflies like, for example, coneflower and buddleia.

ADDING READY-MADE SHUTTERS

*I*n the old days, shutters had a practical purpose—they were needed to help keep out the cold and protect the windows during storms. By happy accident, those shutters looked great when they were left open.

Today storm windows and insulated glass provide better protection from the cold without darkening the house, but the old-fashioned look of shutters is still appealing. That's why so many houses have nonfunctioning shutters attached to the sides of their windows.

With shutters, you can quickly define a new look for a plain exterior wall. Louvered shutters lend a period look; other types can incorporate a design of significance to your family, or be in keeping with the style of your home. For decorative touches, cut out patterns like the ones shown on page 99.

Call home centers and lumber yards in your area to find who has a good selection of shutters. There will be a limited number of sizes and styles. Vinyl shutters cannot be painted and will crack with age, but for many years they will be maintenance free. You may be able to custom-order shutters. Before you do, consider making your own (pages 97–99); that way, you can personalize the design.

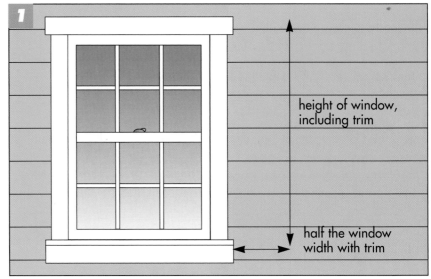

1. Measure for the best look.
Be sure the shutters you choose or make are at least fairly close to the correct size, so that theoretically, if they were used as real shutters, they would cover the window when closed. Otherwise, they will look awkward. This means that each shutter should cover half of the window including the trim.

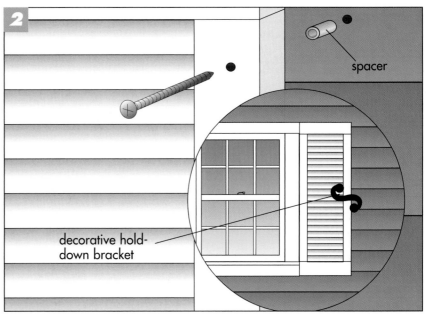

2. Use spacers when attaching.
If a wooden shutter is attached directly to the house, water will be trapped between the shutter and the house, which may very well cause rot within a few years. Mount the shutter away from the house by about half an inch, so that water can run through and allow both the house and the shutter to dry out.

To do this, use spacers made of nonrusting material, such as copper or aluminum pipe, or four or five zinc washers. Drill pilot holes and start driving all the screws, until they poke through a half inch or so. Slip the spacers onto the protruding screws, and have a helper hold the shutter in place as you drive the screws home.

YOU'LL NEED

TIME: An hour to install a pair of shutters.
SKILLS: Leveling, driving screws.
TOOLS: Level, drill.

MAKING YOUR OWN SHUTTERS

Because today shutters are only decorative, they are simple to build. On the next three pages you will find several plans, as well as some cutout designs. Use these as springboards for your own ideas. Choose a style that goes well with your house, and design window boxes and planters at the same time as the shutters (see pages 66–67).

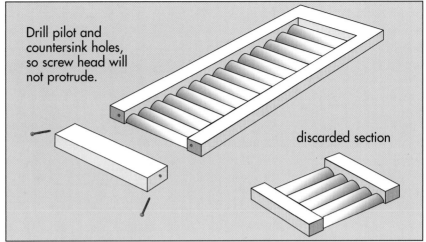

Drill pilot and countersink holes, so screw head will not protrude.

discarded section

YOU'LL NEED

TIME: For most designs, several hours per pair of shutters.
SKILLS: Measuring and squaring, cutting with a circular saw, attaching with screws or nails.
TOOLS: Circular saw, square, drill, hammer, tape measure.

Modify a louvered door.
A little ingenuity may save you a lot of time. Here is one example of how you can adapt ready-made materials for a new use.

Louvered doors are most commonly available as bifold doors for closets, and are available in a variety of widths. Cut the two side framing pieces to the length

you want, minus the width of the bottom framing piece. Separate the bottom piece from the discarded section by tapping with a hammer; use a scrap of wood to prevent dents. Working on a flat surface, reattach the bottom piece by drilling pilot and countersink holes and angle-driving screws.

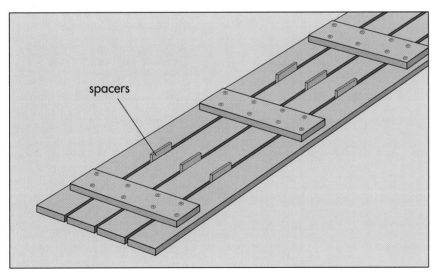

spacers

Try a rustic design.
You may want to use old, weathered boards for this one; just be sure you have enough so that all the shutters on your house look the same. Cut 1×4s, 1×6s, or 1×8s to length, and lay them on a flat, well-swept surface. Check for square, and use spacers to maintain consistent gaps between the boards. Cut crosspieces that

are an inch or two shorter than the width of the shutter. Space them consistently and squarely, and attach with two fasteners per joint in an alternating pattern to avoid splitting a board. It will be easier to fasten with 1¼-inch deck screws, but to achieve a more rustic look, use galvanized nails instead.

EXPERTS' INSIGHT

PAINTING AND TREATING
■ The shutters will probably be exposed to both moisture and intense heat at various times of the year, so prevent further problems by doing a thorough job of finishing them. If you use the louvered-door design (above), take special care, because the panels are made of wood that will rot very quickly if exposed to moisture.
■ Paint is the best finish. Use a high-quality latex exterior paint. Depending on the material, it may be a good idea to apply a coat of stain-killing primer before painting. Brush on at least two coats before you install shutters on your house.

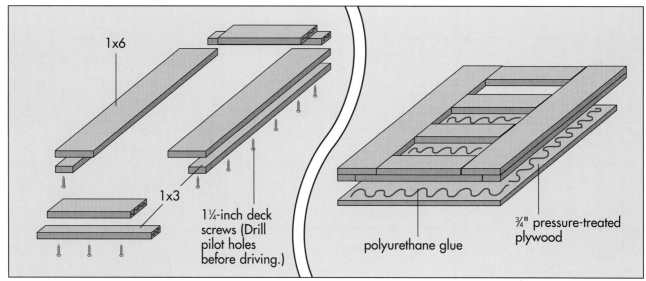

1x6

1x3

1¼-inch deck
screws (Drill
pilot holes
before driving.)

polyurethane glue

¾" pressure-treated
plywood

Constructing paneled shutters.
One way of getting a paneled look
would be to use paneled bifold
closet doors, modifying them
according to the directions for the
louvered shutters on page 97.

If you want to make your own
paneled shutters, use pieces of
1× pressure-treated lumber and
¾-inch pressure-treated plywood.
Cut 1×6s and 1×3s to the height
of the shutter, 1×3s to its width,
and 1×6s to the width minus two
widths of 1×6. Join the pieces
together with polyurethane glue
and 1¼-inch deck screws to form
solidly laminated framing pieces
with edges flush on one side.

Check for square and join
the pieces to each other in the
same manner.

Cut the plywood to fit in back,
inside the 1×3s, and attach with
glue and screws. Attach additional
horizontal 1×6 pieces, evenly
spaced in the middle.

MATCHING SHUTTERS AND WINDOW BOXES

You will not want an ensemble
like this on every window,
but one or two can give a house
real curb appeal. Plan with the
whole house in mind: The shutters
might all be the same, or choose
to have the other shutters in the
same style but without the
decorative cutouts. For window
box designs, see pages 66–67.

Start with the panel shutters,
shown above (omitting the
horizontal middle pieces), or use
the rustic design shutters on page
97. Cut out the patterns using a
sabersaw with a fine-cutting
scrolling blade. Have extra blades
on hand; you will probably break
some. To begin the cut, drill a
hole with a bit large enough to
accommodate your blade. Apply
plenty of paint to the cut-out
areas, because the exposed open
grain will be very susceptible to
moisture damage.

HOW TO TRANSFER A TEMPLATE

Choose a pattern, and decide how large you want it to be—how tall the tulip should be, for instance. Take this book to a copy center, and make a copy of this page. Cut out the design you want, and enlarge it to the size you want. You will probably have to experiment and recopy at various enlargement percentages until you get just what you want. Cut the enlarged pattern out with scissors and carefully position it on your shutter, then trace the outline for cutting with a sabersaw.

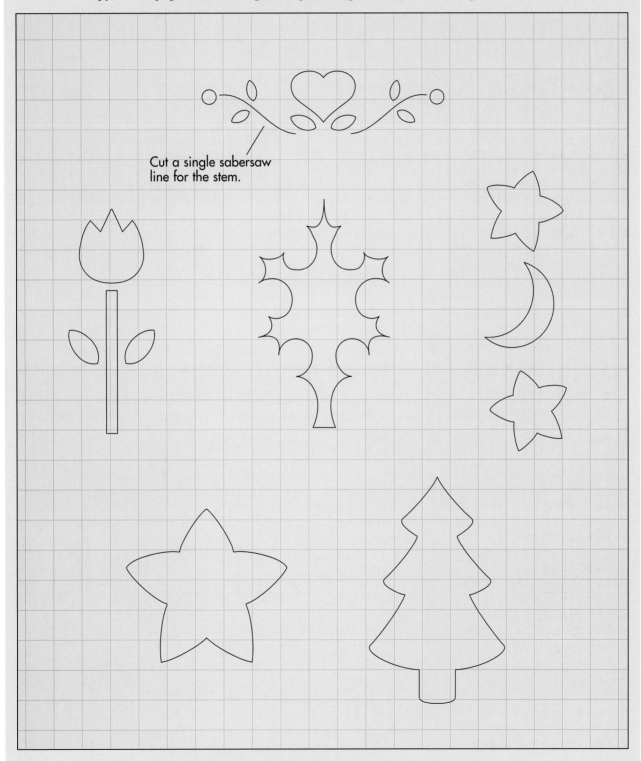

Cut a single sabersaw line for the stem.

BUILDING A DRY CREEK AND BRIDGE

This unusual feature lends rustic charm to a larger yard. It can serve as a divider between two spaces, both separating them and bridging them at the same time.

If you do have a small body of water, this structure can work as a literal bridge. Soak the posts that will sit in the water in extra preservative, and pound them into the creek bed with a sledge hammer until you hit something solid, or until they are sunk 4 feet into the mud.

YOU'LL NEED

TIME: With two helpers, several days to dig the creek and build the bridge.
SKILLS: Excavating, transporting and arranging rocks, good carpentry.
TOOLS: Shovels, posthole digger, wheelbarrow, level, handsaw, circular saw, drill, hammer, string line, square.

1. Excavate the dry creek.
This may be the most difficult part of the job. If you already have a depression on your property, you may need only remove all sod and plants. If there is a lot of digging to do, contact a landscaping contractor, rent a small earth-moving machine, or hire out this back-straining part of the job.

Using garden hoses, flour, or sand, lay out the desired shape for your creek bed. Remove all roots and other organic materials. You may be able to mound the soil on the sides, eliminating having to haul away the soil.

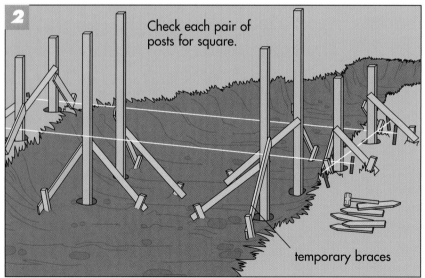

Check each pair of posts for square.

temporary braces

2. Set the posts.
Use two string lines spanning the creek to mark for the posts. Widthwise, make the posts no more than 3 feet apart, from outside of post to outside of post. Run perpendicular string lines and check each pair of postholes for square, using the 3-4-5 method (page 13).

Dig postholes at least 30 inches deep, shovel in a few inches of gravel, and set the posts in. Check each for plumb in both directions, and recheck for square. Anchor them temporarily with braces.

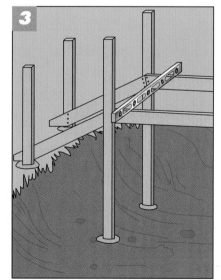

3. Install framing.
Install 2×6s to the inside of the posts. (If any span is over 8 feet, use 2×8s.) Check the middle pieces for level in both directions; the ramp pieces should be parallel to each other in height. Pour concrete into the postholes.

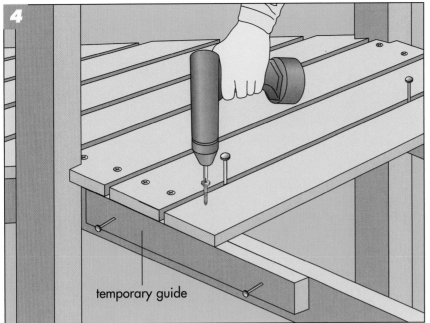

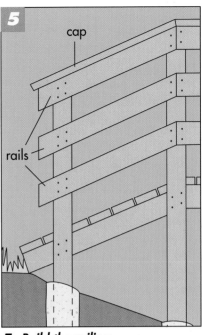

4. Lay the decking.

Gang-cut 2×6 decking pieces, 3 inches longer than the distance from outside to outside of the framing pieces. (If your framing varies by an inch or so, that does not matter.) On the outside of one 2×6, temporarily place a 2× piece of lumber to use as a guide. To install the decking, check for square with a framing square, hold the decking piece flush to the face of the 2× guide, and drive two 3-inch deck screws at each joint. Use nails as spacers between the decking pieces. When you come to a post, hold in place and mark for notches; cut them with a circular saw and a handsaw.

5. Build the railing.

Cut the posts to height—40 inches is recommended. Use a level and a long board to mark for three evenly spaced rails, and install the rails with at least two 3-inch deck screws at each joint. Use a T-bevel to mark for odd angle cuts. Add a 2×6 cap, laid flat on the top rail.

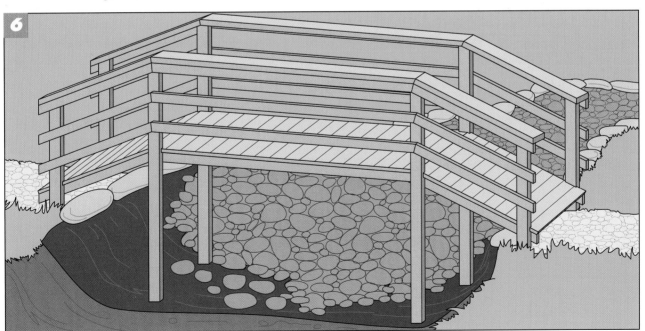

6. Lay a stone creekbed.

Lay two or more layers of landscaping fabric in the creekbed; allow it to run up on the sides so you can cut it later. Fill the bed with rocks of various sizes. Aim at a fairly even distribution of large and small rocks. Place large stones at the top of the creek bank over the fabric. Then trim the fabric. You may also want to lay a stone or concrete paver path leading to the bridge in both directions.

ADDING A WATER GARDEN

Once an extravagance available only to the wealthy, garden pools are now affordable and buildable for most any homeowner. A pool will enable you to bring exciting new species of plants and animals into your backyard.

You can make a simple and small reflecting pond by digging a hole and setting a galvanized horse trough in it. (Troughs are available at farm supply houses and some home centers.) Add a recirculating pump to keep the water aerated. The project presented here is more elaborate, and allows you to choose your own shape and size.

This is a big project. You may want to hire some of the digging done for you.

If possible, choose a flat spot for the pool—remember that the rim of the pool must be level. A spot in the sun rather than under a tree will keep the water warmer, and you won't have to clean out all those leaves.

The right mix of plants and fish will help to keep the pool clean and healthy; however, a pump with a fountain will make your job easier. The fountain adds oxygen and movement to the water—preventing mosquitos and other insects from breeding in the pond. Have an electrician install an outside receptacle with a GFCI outlet, so you can plug in the pump.

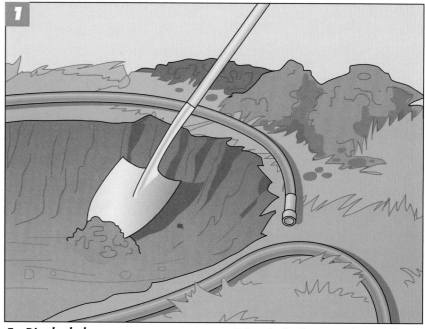

YOU'LL NEED
TIME: Several days, with a helper.
SKILLS: Digging, leveling, laying stones, connecting a pump.
TOOLS: Shovels, rake, hand tamper, wheelbarrow, garden hose, level, scissors.

1. Dig the hole.
Contact your utility companies mark electrical, gas, phone, or water lines. Lay a garden hose on the lawn in the shape of your future pool. Keep the shape fairly simple.

Dig a hole that is at least 2 feet deep. (In areas with cold winters, dig at least 3 feet deep if you want fish to survive.) Completely remove any organic material, roots, and sharp stones.

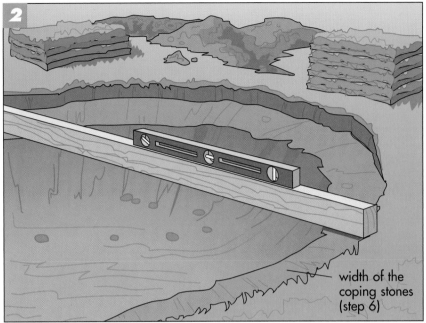

width of the coping stones (step 6)

3. Pack the sides, then add sand.
Use a hand tamper to compact the soil on the sides and bottom of the pool. Make sure there is nothing that could tear the plastic liner (step 4). Shovel sand onto the bottom of the pool, and spread it out with a rake, to about 2 inches thick.

2. Cut sod and level the rim.
Around the edge of the pool, use a square-edged shovel or an edge cutter to neatly remove the sod in a path that is wide enough for the paving materials you will be using (see step 6). •

Use a level set on top of a straight board to see that the pool rim is level all the way around. If needed, remove soil from the high spots, or add soil to a low spot, and tamp firmly.

4. Lay the liner and bricks.
Use pool liner made of PVC plastic or synthetic rubber, at least 45 mils thick. Place it in the middle of the pool bottom and unfold it,

molding it to the shape of the pool as you go. Make sure there is plenty of liner all around the perimeter; it may pull down when you fill the pool.

Use a garden hose to fill the pool with water, and edge the pool with bricks. Cut the liner along the sod line with a pair of scissors.

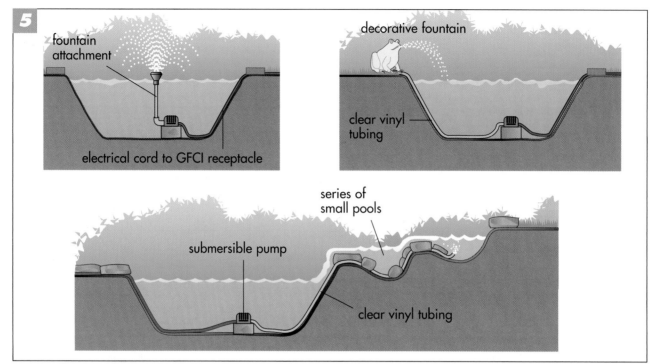

5. Install a water pump.

You have three options: A fountain in the middle of the pond (upper left) can either spray up into the air, or it can be set lower so it just bubbles up and keeps the water in motion. A variety of fountain heads are available.

A decorative fountain placed outside the pool (upper right) recirculates water through a statue of your choice. Use a statue made for the purpose, or think up your own playful design.

A waterfall (bottom) is not as hard to make as it appears. Use the soil that you took out of the pool to create an elevated area with dips. Line the area with a pool liner, and lay smooth rocks over it, taking care not to rip the liner.

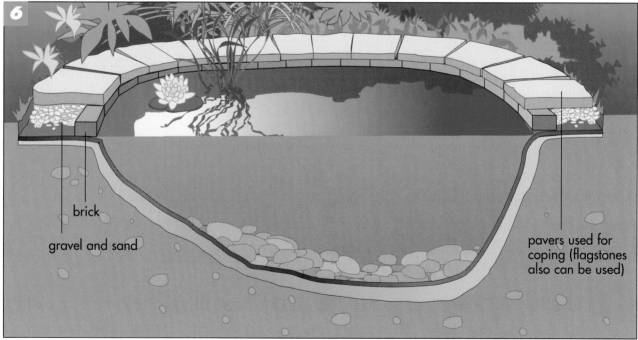

6. Add coping and pebbles.

Behind the bricks, lay a base of gravel and sand; tamp and smooth it. Set the coping stones or pavers so they overhang the bricks by an inch or so. Shovel fine sand into the gaps between the coping stones, and brush with a broom. Wet the surface with a fine mist from a hose, let it dry, and repeat, until the joints stay filled with sand. Layer the bottom of the pool with smooth decorative stones.

7. **Add the right plants and fish.**
Home centers and nurseries carry a variety of plants designed for use in pools. Consult with a knowledgeable salesperson to find the best plants and animals for your area and your type of pool.

It is possible to have plants grow in mud that you add to the bottom of the pool, but keeping the plants in containers is much easier and allows you to move plants around at will. Begin with underwater oxygenating plants, such as milfoil and waterweed. Then add surface plants, such as water lily and water chestnut. You may also want some plants for the edge of the pool: Japanese iris and arrowhead are good choices.

Surprisingly large fish will survive in a garden pond. Goldfish are a good, reasonably priced choice; there are many types, some of which aren't at all golden in color. A few minnows or other small fish can help keep a pool clear of algae and insects. Game fish—catfish, bluegills, and trout, for instance—may work in your area. If you have the time and are sure raccoons cannot reach them, you may want to spend the money for Japanese koi, a kind of carp that live as long as humans and often behave like family pets.

Consult with a dealer and come up with a master plan for your pond's fish and plants. Certain fish will not get along with other types, and some fish will destroy certain types of plants.

CAUTION!
PROTECT YOUR FLORA AND FAUNA
- *Wait a few days before adding plants or fish to your pond, so the chlorine can leach out of the water.*
- *Slowly acclimate your fish to the water's temperature before you put them in. If you have trouble with raccoons or other predators, provide a place for the fish to hide, such as overhanging flagstones around the edge.*
- *Every three to four years, remove all the plants and fish and drain the pond. Clean the liner thoroughly, and perhaps replace the pump.*

BUILDING A FIRE PIT

This is really two projects in one—a fire pit, and a patio surface. If you already have a patio surface, remove pavers to make a 3-foot-square opening, and dig for the fire pit. You may need to cut pavers with a circular saw equipped with a masonry blade.

This project is designed to minimize risk, but fire is always a force to be reckoned with. Cut away any low-hanging nearby branches, keep the area clear of flammable substances, and teach children about fire safety.

Bricklaying is a skill that takes years to learn properly. But on this project, the mortar joints will be barely visible.

YOU'LL NEED

TIME: Several days, with a helper.
SKILLS: Bricklaying, measuring and excavating, laying pavers.
TOOLS: Circular saw, shovel, mallet, drill, wheelbarrow, mason's trowel, push broom.

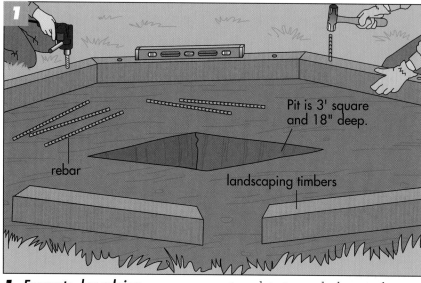

Pit is 3' square and 18" deep.

rebar

landscaping timbers

1. Excavate, lay edging.
Determine the dimensions and shape of your patio (10 feet square is a good size). Cut landscaping timbers to form the perimeter of the patio; you will need to cut two sides with a circular saw, and perhaps finish cutting the middle with a handsaw. Set the timbers in place on the yard, and use them as a template to mark the area by cutting the sod with a shovel.

Remove the timbers and excavate the patio area to a depth of 4 inches. In the middle, dig a hole 3 feet square and 18 inches deep. Set the timbers back in place, and anchor them by drilling holes and driving 3-foot sections of reinforcing bar into the ground.

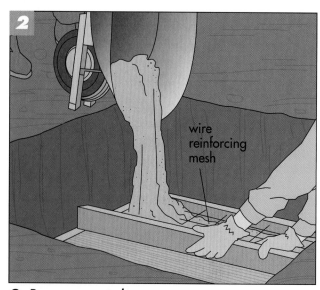

wire reinforcing mesh

2. Pour a concrete base.
Tamp the bottom of the hole firm, shovel in several inches of gravel, and tamp again. Make a form by anchoring 2×4s to stakes, and check for level. Cut wire reinforcing mesh to fit, and pour 3 inches of concrete. Use a straight board to level the base.

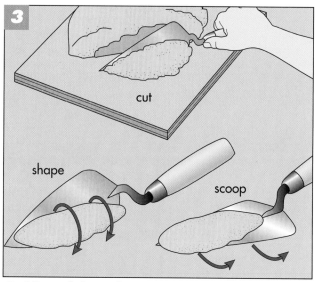

cut

shape

scoop

3. Mix and shape the mortar.
In a wheelbarrow, combine mortar mix with water until it sticks to a trowel when turned upside-down. Shovel the mortar onto a board. Slice off a piece and shape it so it is about the size and shape of the trowel. Scoop it up with a smooth sweep, giving a slight upward jerk to make the mortar stick firmly.

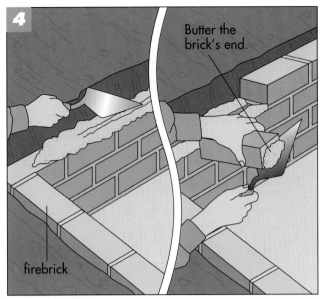

4. Lay the firebricks.

Brick laying is a time-consuming job, so don't rush. Lay out lines on the base. Spread mortar to an even thickness, then lightly draw the point of the trowel across the mortar to make a furrow. Butter one end of each brick (except the first one) before setting in mortar. Check with a level from time to time. Lay the courses with alternating joint lines. Cut bricks with a chisel or by striking with the trowel. Build up the wall until it is the height of the future patio.

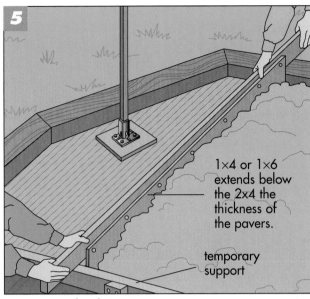

5. Prepare for the pavers.

Tamp the soil firm in the patio area, and cover it with landscaping fabric. Pour in enough sand to cover the area to a depth of 2 inches or so depending on the thickness of your pavers. Make a screed out of a straight 2×4 with a length of 1×4 or 1×6 nailed to it. With a helper, work the screed back and forth as you move it sideways to achieve a level surface. For sections wider than 8 feet, install a temporary support. Tamp the sand firm, add a bit more sand, and screed again.

6. Lay the pavers.

Start in a corner and set the bricks in place, taking care not to disturb the level sand surface. Set each paver snugly against its neighbor. Check for straightness with a string line every fourth course. After the bricks are laid, brush fine sand into the joints, spray with a fine mist, and repeat.

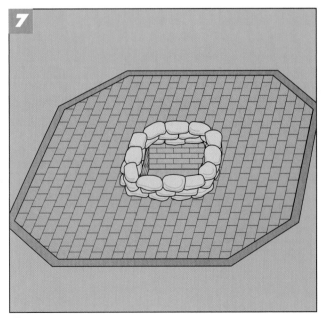

7. Lay a stone cap.

To finish the fire pit, mix some more mortar. Lay a thick bed on top of the fire bricks and the patio surface, and set decorative stones in it. Build up the stone cap to a height of a foot or more, setting each course of stone in mortar.

GLOSSARY

For words not listed here, or for more about those that are, refer to the index, pages 110–112.

Actual dimension. The true size of a piece of lumber, after milling and drying. *See also* Nominal dimension.

Batter board. A board frame supported by stakes set back from the corners of a structure. Saw kerfs or marks on the boards indicate the location of the edges of the footings and the structure, which can be used to reposition those points on the site following its excavation.

Beam. A large horizontal framing piece, usually made of 4× or doubled 2× lumber, which usually rests on posts and is used to support joists.

Bearing wall. An interior or exterior wall that helps support the roof or the floor joists above.

Bevel cut. A cut made at an angle through the thick dimension of a piece of wood.

Building codes. Community ordinances governing the manner in which a home or other structure may be constructed or modified. Most codes deal primarily with fire and health concerns and have separate sections relating to electrical, plumbing, and structural work.

Butt joint. The joint formed by two pieces of material when fastened end to end, end to face, or end to edge.

Caulk. Any of a variety of different compounds used to seal seams and joints against infiltration of water and air.

Concrete. A building and paving material made by mixing water with sand, gravel, and cement. *See also* Mortar.

Countersink. To drive in the head of a nail or screw so its top is flush with the surface of the surrounding wood.

Crosscut. To saw a piece of lumber perpendicular to its length and/or its grain.

Decking. The boards used to make the walking surface of a deck. Decking is usually made of 2×6, 2×4, or ⁵⁄₄×6 lumber.

Edging. Pieces of wood used to cover the edges of boards, especially decking boards.

Dimension lumber. A piece of lumber that is 2 inches thick and at least 2 inches wide.

Drywall. A basic interior building material consisting of big sheets of pressed gypsum faced with heavy paper on both sides. Also known as gypsum board, plasterboard, and Sheetrock (a trade name).

End grain. The ends of wood fibers, which are exposed at the ends of boards.

Finial. An decorative element, often a ball or cone, attached to the top of a stair, porch, deck post, or roof gable.

Flush. On the same plane as, or level with, a surrounding surface.

Footing. A small foundation, usually made of concrete, used to support a post.

Frost·heave. The upthrust of soil caused when moist soil freezes. Posts and footings that do not extend below the frost line are subject to frost heave.

Grain. The direction and pattern of fibers in a piece of wood.

Hardwood. Lumber that comes from leaved, deciduous trees, such as oak and maple.

Inside corner. The point at which two walls form an internal angle, as in the corner of a room.

Joists. Horizontal framing members that support a floor and/or ceiling.

Joist hanger. A metal piece of connector used to join a joist and a ledger or rim joist, so that their top edges are flush.

Lag screw. A screw, usually ¼ inch in diameter or larger, with a hexagonal head that can be driven with a wrench or socket.

Lattice. A type of fence or screening made of crisscrossed pieces of wood.

Ledger. A horizontal strip (typically lumber) that's used to provide support for the ends or edges of other members.

Level. The condition that exists when any type of surface is at true horizontal. Also a tool used to determine level.

Linear foot. A term used to refer to the length of a board or piece of molding, in contrast to board foot.

Miter joint. The joint formed when two boards or pieces of trim meet that have been cut at the same angle (usually 45°).

Masonry cement. A special mix of portland cement and hydrated lime used for preparing mortar. The lime adds to the workability of the mortar.

Miter joint. The joint formed when two members meet that have been cut at the same angle, usually 45 degrees.

Molding. A strip of wood, usually small-dimensioned, used to cover exposed edges or as decoration.

Mortar. A mixture of masonry cement, masonry sand, and water. For most jobs, the proportion of cement to sand is 1:3.

Nailer. A length of board into which nails or screws can be fastened when the thickness or position of a member makes fastening difficult.

Nominal dimension. The stated size of a piece of lumber, such as a 2×4 or a 1×12. The actual dimension is somewhat smaller.

On-center (OC). A phrase used to designate the distance from the center of one regularly spaced framing member to the center of the next one.

Outside corners. The point at which two walls form an external angle, the corner you can usually walk around.

Particle board. Panels made from compressed wood chips and glue.

Pier. A vertical piece of concrete, used as a footing to support a post. Make your own pier by pouring concrete, or purchase a ready-made concrete pier.

Pilot hole. A small hole drilled into a wooden member to avoid splitting the wood when driving a screw or nail.

Plumb. The condition that exists when a member is at true vertical.

Plumb bob. Weight used with a plumb line to align vertical points.

Plywood. A building material made of sheets of wood veneer glued together with the grains at 90-degree angles to each other.

Post. A vertical framing piece, usually 4×4 or 6×6, used to support a beam or a joist.

Post top. A flat piece of wood, often with routed edges, fastened to a post to protect the end grain.

Pressure-treated wood. Lumber and sheet goods impregnated with one of several solutions to make the wood virtually impervious to moisture and weather.

Ready-mix. Concrete that is mixed in a truck as it is being transported to the job site.

Rebar (reinforcing rod). Steel rod that is used to reinforce concrete and masonry structures.

Reinforcing wire mesh. A steel screening used to reinforce certain types of concrete projects, such as walks, drives, and patios.

Rip. To saw lumber or sheet goods parallel to the grain pattern.

Sealer. A protective, usually clear, coating applied to wood or metal.

Setback. The minimum distance between a property line and any structure, as delimited by local building departments.

Span. The distance traveled by a beam, joist, or decking board between supporting structures.

Softwood. Lumber derived from evergreen conifers, such as pine and fir.

Square. The condition that exists when one surface is at a 90-degree

angle to another. Also a tool used to determine square.

Straightedge. An improvised tool, usually a 1×4 or 2×4 with a straight edge, used to mark a straight line on material or to determine if a surface is even.

Studs. Vertical 2×4 or 2×6 framing members spaced at regular intervals within a wall

Template. A pattern cut from wood, paper, or other material that serves as a guide for certain cutting tools.

Three-four-five method. An easy, mathematical way to check whether a large angle is square. Measure 3 feet along one side, 4 feet along the other; if the corner is square, the diagonal distance between those two points will equal 5 feet.

Toenail. To drive a nail at an angle, so as to hold together two pieces of material.

Tongue-and-groove. Flooring or siding boards that have a projecting tongue on one edge and a corresponding groove on the opposite edge.

Trowel. Any of several flat and oblong or flat and pointed metal tools used for finishing and/or handling concrete and mortar.

Warp. Any of several lumber defects caused by uneven shrinkage of wood cells.

Yard. A unit of volume in which ready-mix concrete is sold; equal to 1 square yard (27 cubic feet).

Zoning. Ordinances regulating the ways in which a property may be used in any given neighborhood. Zoning laws may limit where you can locate a structure. *See also* Building codes.

INDEX

METRIC CONVERSIONS

U.S. UNITS TO METRIC EQUIVALENTS			METRIC UNITS TO U.S. EQUIVALENTS		
To Convert From	Multiply By	To Get	To Convert From	Multiply By	To Get
Inches	25.4	Millimeters	Millimeters	0.0394	Inches
Inches	2.54	Centimeters	Centimeters	0.3937	Inches
Feet	30.48	Centimeters	Centimeters	0.0328	Feet
Feet	0.3048	Meters	Meters	3.2808	Feet
Yards	0.9144	Meters	Meters	1.0936	Yards
Miles	1.6093	Kilometers	Kilometers	0.6214	Miles
Square inches	6.4516	Square centimeters	Square centimeters	0.1550	Square inches
Square feet	0.0929	Square meters	Square meters	10.764	Square feet
Square yards	0.8361	Square meters	Square meters	1.1960	Square yards
Acres	0.4047	Hectares	Hectares	2.4711	Acres
Square miles	2.5899	Square kilometers	Square kilometers	0.3861	Square miles
Cubic inches	16.387	Cubic centimeters	Cubic centimeters	0.0610	Cubic inches
Cubic feet	0.0283	Cubic meters	Cubic meters	35.315	Cubic feet
Cubic feet	28.316	Liters	Liters	0.0353	Cubic feet
Cubic yards	0.7646	Cubic meters	Cubic meters	1.308U	Cubic yards
Cubic yards	764.55	Liters	Liters	0.0013	Cubic yards
Fluid ounces	29.574	Milliliters	Milliliters	0.0338	Fluid ounces
Quarts	0.9464	Liters	Liters	1.0567	Quarts
Gallons	3.7854	Liters	Liters	0.2642	Gallons
Drams	1.7718	Grams	Grams	0.5644	Drams
Ounces	28.350	Grams	Grams	0.0353	Ounces
Pounds	0.4536	Kilograms	Kilograms	2.2046	Pounds
To convert from degrees Fahrenheit (F) to degrees Celsius (C), first subtract 32, then multiply by $\frac{5}{9}$.			To convert from degrees Celsius to degrees Fahrenheit, multiply by $\frac{9}{5}$, then add 32.		